THE EXORCIST

William Peter Blatty

ff

faber and faber

First published in 1998
by Faber and Faber Limited
Bloomsbury House
74-77 Great Russell Street
London, WC1B 3DA

Photoset by Parker Typesetting Service, Leicester
Printed and bound by CPI Group (UK) Ltd, Croydon, CR0 4YY

A CIP record for this book
is available from the British Library

ISBN 9780571202393

Kathy Galloway * Margaret Hebblethwaite
Nicholas King SJ * Bede Leach OSB
Esther Mombo * Martin Warner

Facing forward

Reflections on the Scripture Readings for Lent 2006

Christian Aid

DARTON·LONGMAN+TODD

First published in Great Britain in 2006 by

CAFOD
Romero Close, Stockwell Road, London SW9 9TY

Christian Aid
35 Lower Marsh, Waterloo, London SE1 7RT

Darton, Longman and Todd Ltd
1 Spencer Court, 140–142 Wandsworth High Street
London SW18 4JJ

ISBN 0 232 52647 8

Note: the Hebrew numbering of the Psalms is used. From Psalm 10 to 147 this is ahead of the Greek and Vulgate numbering which is used in some psalters.

Cover photo: Annie Bungeroth/CAFOD
Cover design: Garry Lambert

Text designed and produced by Sandie Boccacci
Set in 9.5/13pt Palatino
Printed and bound in Great Britain by Cox and Wyman

Contents

About the authors

Kathy Galloway is the Leader of the Iona Community. She is an ordained minister of the Church of Scotland, a practical theologian, campaigner and the author of several books on theology and spirituality, including *Struggles to Love: The Spirituality of the Beatitudes.*

Margaret Hebblethwaite is the former Assistant Editor of the international Catholic weekly, *The Tablet*, and the author of several books, including *Motherhood and God.* Since 2000 she has lived and worked in the rural village of Santa Maria de Fe in Paraguay.

Nicholas King SJ lived and worked in South Africa for twelve years, and is currently teaching New Testament at Oxford.

Bede Leach OSB is a monk of Ampleforth Abbey.

Esther Mombo is Academic Dean of St Paul's United Theological Seminary, Limuru, Kenya. She was a member of the Lambeth Commission on Communion which produced *The Windsor Report 2004.*

Martin Warner is the Canon Pastor at St Paul's Cathedral, London; he was previously the administrator of the shrine at Walsingham. He is the author of *Known to the Senses: Five Days of the Passion.*

Introduction

'Who will roll away the stone?' the women asked on the first Easter day. In her reflections Margaret Hebblethwaite reminds us that the martyred Jesuit theologian, Ignacio Ellacuría, used to call the poor 'the crucified peoples' and the heavy, apparently unbudgeable stone at the entrance to Jesus' tomb evokes the spirit-crushing work of so many in the world.

According to the UN, the world's 500 richest people have a combined income greater than that of the poorest 416 million. We are one human family, equally loved and precious in the eyes of God. Yet four out of ten of us are living on less than $2 a day, while four out of ten of us would think little of spending that on a cappuccino.

Nicholas King reflects on the story of the Transfiguration, a glimpse, in the middle of Lent, of the resurrection of Jesus, so impossibly hard to imagine in the cruel mess of our world. We live and work and pray in the present, but in Lent, in particular, we face forwards, towards the moment when the stone will be rolled away.

We wait not only for the resurrection of Jesus, but for the resurrection of the poor. 'As Christ was raised from the dead by the Father's glory' so too will the crucified peoples inherit new life.

BRENDAN WALSH

Facing forward

The CAFOD/Christian Aid/DLT Lent Book 2006

Martin Warner

Ash Wednesday to Saturday after Ash Wednesday

Ash Wednesday

Ambassadors for Christ

Jl 2:12–18; Ps 51; Co 5:20–6:2; Mt 6:1–6, 16–18

> *'I have loved you with an everlasting love; and so I still maintain my faithful love for you.'* (Jeremiah 31:3)

We don't like being labelled but we do like badges. What's the difference?

I suppose labels are the uninvited statements that people attach to us and we resent that, understandably. But at the same time we are increasingly happy to wear self-chosen labels, badges that say what we want to say about ourselves.

Some of these badges are now a fashion-accessory. The white *Make Poverty History* armbands, wristbands, neck bands and other bands were a must-have of the summer of 2005. It was like saying, 'If I write this and wear it, I commit myself to it wherever I am.' That is very scriptural.

Exodus tells us that the vestments that Aaron and his descendents wore had two stones, carnelians, engraved with the names of the tribes of Israel and mounted in gold settings on the shoulder straps. This meant that Aaron would 'bear their names before the Lord on his two shoulders for remembrance' (see Exodus 28).

Last year's exhibition at the Tate Modern of art by Frida Kahlo took this a stage further. There was a quite early self-portrait by Kahlo in which she had painted on her forehead a miniature of Diego Rivera, the man she loved and twice married.

The contemporary artist Tracy Emin commented on this as a painting she both hated and loved: 'I could have had Matt Collishaw tattooed across my whole body at one point. I understand what she was thinking. People would say: "What's on your mind?" And I'd say, "Can't you see who I'm in love with? It's on my forehead."'

On your forehead and mine is invisibly and indelibly marked the baptismal name that we bear before the whole world as the statement of who we are in love with. Jesus Christ is my intimate and my friend as well as being my lord and my God. As Christians we bear his name – literally, like the descendents of Aaron who carried the names of the tribes of Israel to whom they belonged.

And the ashes on my forehead are another manifestation of the name of Jesus. This is the name of those that he most closely resembled in his life on earth; the poor, the homeless, those denied justice, those who sit in the ashes of grief and dispossession.

Today you make a universal and life-changing fashion statement to the world: 'Can't you see who I'm in love with? It's on my forehead.'

Thought for the day

To obtain the gift of holiness is the work of *a life*.

(John Henry Newman 1801–1890)

Prayer

Take away, good Lord, the sin that corrupts us,
give us the sorrow that heals
and the joy that praises
and restore by grace your image within us;
we ask this through Jesus Christ the Lord. Amen.

Clean me!

Dt 30:15–20; Ps 1; Lk 9:22–25

> *'Since by your obedience to the truth you have purified yourselves so that you can experience the genuine love of brothers and sisters, love each other intensely from the heart.'* (1 Peter 1:22)

Stuck in traffic on a busy Thursday, you may spend some considerable time staring at the back of a car or lorry, noticing in the dirt of its rear end an invitation: 'Clean me!'

The grime and pollution that dirties our cars, vans, lorries, or buses is inescapable. One of the tragedies of driving a new car off the sales forecourt is the knowledge that the lovely smell of newness within, and the sparkle of all-over cleanness outside, will not last long, no matter how careful a driver one might be.

Over-attachment to material things is a danger in which cars can feature prominently. The difficulty occurs, I think, when we lend the car a personality of its own – a voice that can say, 'Clean me, cherish me; I'm yours.' The real sting is a competitive, self-serving reference in the voice we have imagined: a clean (sleek, smart, smooth) car makes me feel and look good beside others.

There is a marked contrast here with the way we experience similar language in Psalm 51, one of the penitential psalms frequently used in this season of Lent.

Washing, purging and cleaning feature prominently in the language of this psalm. It is an authentic human voice that cries out from the text. But we might not readily locate the 'Wash me' of the psalmist in the experience of adult life.

When was the last time you were washed by someone else? It is an experience we would generally associate with tenderness and vulnerability. We are washed as tiny children, as patients in hospital, especially after major surgery, as an expression of intimacy and love, and when the frailty of old age demands that we learn dependency on others.

It is often tempting to begin Lent with schemes for spiritual warfare and the disciplining of the flesh and the will; we are talking serious books to read, denial of alcohol, chocolate, meat (extreme), the theatre and cinema (very extreme).

This is all very fine, but are we ready for the simpler, possibly more humbling prayer: 'Wash me'? It's a prayer for the abandonment of our totality into the hands of another in nakedness, perhaps with shame and the humble recognition of some kind of refreshment that is beyond us yet needed by all of us, irrespective of status.

And the sting, the lesson of Lent: cleanliness is not competitive but is characteristic of the freedom that has an unashamed capacity for worship and adoration.

Thought for the day

The fundamental business of life is always worship.

(William Temple 1881–1944)

Prayer

Lord Jesus Christ,
From our youth to our old age,
May we know the strength
of your gentle protection
and the cleansing power
of your compassionate salvation. Amen

Musical scales

Is 58:1–9; Ps 51; Mt 9:14–15

> *'Even the nations are like a drop from a bucket, and are accounted as dust on the scales; see, he takes up the isles like fine dust.'* (Isaiah 40:15)

I remember my tutor telling me when I was a student that one of the highlights of his honeymoon in Italy was a performance of Verdi's Requiem.

At the time this seemed eccentric. But many years later a performance of that same work filled me with a profound sense of passion, tenderness and self-revelation.

The vast scale of Verdi's music puts a disturbing question: What do you know about death and the scales of judgement?

For the most part we know little about death today and the process of death is well managed. Rarely does it happen at home. At the hospice or hospital there are people to help us through and care for the details.

There is little reticence about death in Verdi's requiem. The trumpets that announce the day of judgement seem to blow from heaven itself, and the inspiration for that is to be found in the text of the *Dies irae* (Day of Wrath) itself.

Here death is the prelude to the invasive experience of judgement in which our inner secrets are revealed; 'Lo, the book exactly worded, wherein all hath been recorded; thence shall judgement be awarded.' Taken on its own this could indeed be a fearsome prospect. But Verdi also presents us with music of love and tenderness, another element in the text: 'Lord, all-pitying, Jesu blest, grant them thine eternal rest.'

Today's gospel reading also draws together themes of death, judgement and tenderness. In response to a question from the disciples of John the Baptist Jesus speaks of fasting as a kind of mourning. Fasting is the freely chosen moment of dying to the satisfaction of our hunger and bodily want.

John the Baptist had turned the attention of his hearers to judgement. But when the judge comes we discover that he is also the bridegroom, prompting John the Baptist to declare (in John's version of the arrival of Jesus) 'the bridegroom's friend, who stands there and listens to him, is filled with joy at the bridegroom's voice. This is the joy I feel.'

Jesus the judge and bridegroom brings the light of truth. This is not the instrument of forensic inquiry, but an expression of desire – to know all that there is about another person. The passion that burns within the divine lover cannot be diminished by anything that truth brings to light; it can only love the lacerations of our guilt into the unexpected beauty of wounds that have been healed.

Thought for the day

Christian redemption is God's Mercy to all Mankind.

(William Law 1686–1761)

Prayer

Almighty Lord and Saviour,
behold with pity the wounds of your people;
do not forsake us, sinful as we are,
but for the sake of the passion of your Beloved One, Jesus Christ,
come quickly to our aid. Amen.

Letter skills

Is 58:9–14; Ps 86:1–6; Lk 5:27–32

Look, I have engraved you on the palms of my hands.
(Isaiah 49:16)

A friend of mine describes herself as an alphabetician. She doesn't just write the letters of the alphabet, she engraves them in stone. But not just any old letters; there are many ways of forming them, and each way has its own character.

An alphabetician works with public words, knowing how to fit a style to a particular need because she or he writes in stone to commemorate many different types of event. A marriage, an anniversary, the opening of a new hospital – these are all things to celebrate.

But there are more sombre moments to commemorate. These moments are caught in words that hold our memories. The character of both inscription and the letters used is part of how an alphabetician catches the narration of a life ended and a grief in search of words.

Like many of God's gifts to us, letters are raw material. We are also given the freedom and creative capacity to work them into a language by which, before God, we express pain, beauty, hope, prayer, humour, sorrow, love, recognition, surrender.

This gift of letters was imaginatively acknowledged in the way that churches used to be consecrated. It took a very long time. Quite early on in the day, as the service got going, the Bishop traced with the tip of his pastoral staff the letters first of the Latin, then of the Greek alphabets in two intersecting diagonal lines made of ash, stretching across the whole body of the church.

We haven't quite lost the hang of how important this formation of words is for us. When I visit the homes of my friends who have young children, and some who don't, I often see those fridge magnets that are a series of letters and words, presenting the invitation to become an alphabetician.

Scripture presents a similar invitation. The prophets construct strange names to illustrate their message: 'Not-my-people' and 'I-am-not-yours' (Hosea 1) is an anguished construction about alienation from God; 'Repairer-of-the-breach' and 'Restorer-of-the-streets-to-live-in' (Isaiah 58) is the hint of what might be, if justice were rightly served.

Just as our homes are places in which we foster the skill of the alphabetician, so too must our churches be places in which this craft is practiced. From the letters once – notionally – etched in ash upon the dedicated threshold we have the task of forming the gospel language of life and freedom for the whole human race.

Thought for the day

Love is made known in fidelity, in devotion, and in witness, and above all in making Christ known, in expanding his life, that is, in becoming his body.

(Sr Agatha Mary SPB)

Prayer

God our Father,
you have spoken through your word, Jesus Christ,
the light who shines in our darkened world.
By the power of the Spirit he bequeathed to us
may we make known your grace
and walk in the ways of your justice and peace,
for your name's sake. Amen.

Martin Warner

First Week of Lent

First Sunday of Lent

Monkey business

Gn 9:8–15; Ps 25:4–9; 1 P 3:18–22; Mk 1:12–15

> *God said, 'I now set my bow in the clouds and it shall be a sign of the Covenant between me and the earth.'*
>
> (Genesis 9:13)

In the wilderness Jesus met a monkey.

The monkey was contemptuous of this invasion of a terrain better suited to non-human species and decided to teach the visitor a lesson about the superior wilderness skills of the monkeys.

'I can climb higher, run faster and jump further than you,' said the monkey. Jesus said nothing.

'I said, I can climb higher, run faster and jump further than you,' gabbled the monkey, flustered by the lack of any response. 'In fact, I'll show you.'

And with that the monkey hurtled into the air and completed a massive leap onto the other side of the ravine in which they had met.

Scampering back, the monkey expected some kind of reaction. Jesus said nothing.

Unable to bear the silence the monkey snapped, 'OK, so you want more? I'll show you more.' Running up to a precipice, swinging across the ravine but barely touching the other side, in one huge bound it crossed to the mouth of the far distant caves sometimes visited by intrepid humans seeking solitude.

The journey back took a bit longer. By now the monkey expected at least a flicker of admiration. Jesus said nothing.

So the monkey got really angry and ran four times up and down the slope to the brow of the hill that looked south to Jerusalem, catapulting itself the fifth time into the air, virtually flying across a great tract of desert, right to the very edge of the world.

It was still and eerie at the edge of the world, where there was nothing except four huge columns and an open space, criss-crossed with lines. On the ground in front of the columns the monkey scrawled its name in huge letters, and then lumbered back to the wilderness with an air of satisfaction.

'I have jumped from here to the edge of the world,' said the monkey. 'Beat that!'

Jesus smiled because he loved monkeys and their comic posturing. With considerable effort and pain he slowly stretched out his hand and opened it for the monkey to inspect. It was injured, bruised and bloodstained. Through the dirt you could see that in the palm of the hand someone had written a name.

It was a name that the monkey knew only too well.

And the monkey learnt why to be silent.

'The spirit drove Jesus out into the wilderness … he was with the wild beasts, and the angels looked after him' (Mark 1:12-13).

Thought for the day

It was love which first prompted you to create us.

(Catherine of Siena, *c.* 1347–1380)

Prayer

Free us, God of mercy, from all that keeps us from you,
relieve the misery of the anxious and the ashamed
and fill us with the hope of peace. Amen.

Taking the chair

Lv 19:1–2, 11–18; Ps 19; Mt 35:31–46

> *I saw the Lord seated on a high and lofty throne; his train filled the sanctuary.* (Isaiah 6:1)

There's a chair I'd love to have that's in the shop selling office furniture near me. It's lime green. It's a desk chair. And it costs £750.

Let's not be distracted by cost or status and just focus on furniture.

First of all, chairs are characteristic of homes, offices, cinemas, theatres and very expensive places on air-planes. There exist, even in our hugely affluent part of the world, people who simply do not have access to a chair in these contexts. If they sit, it is on the pavement or a park bench.

What then of chairs in our homes – dining chairs, arm-chairs, kitchen chairs? This list itself suggests a standard of housing and life-style that is characteristic of fewer and fewer people, and not necessarily as a result of their design choice.

To some extent this shift is driven by changing patterns of life. We are far less likely to sit together on chairs around a table, and the notion of a place for the head of the household would seem distinctly odd in today's culture.

Even so this supposes a choice over whether you have table and chairs at which to eat. Increasingly, those who live in rented accommodation ironically spoken of as social housing experience levels of overcrowding that exclude this possibility.

At this point a small voice nags at me, 'But in African villages they live in huts and aren't used to chairs.' This crudely popular statement, ignoring the detail of shanty-towns, post-colonial slum dwellings, and semi-permanent refugee camps, rather makes my point: a chair, especially 'my chair' is an indication of privilege.

So who, then, sits? Quite properly, this is something that is characteristic of the description of God. One version of Psalm 22 describes God as 'enthroned on the praises of Israel.' And Matthew's parable of the Great Assize begins with the image of the glorified Son of Man who 'will take his seat on his throne of glory.'

This is why the image of Jesus bound and standing before the judgement seat of Pilate is so amazing; God incarnate stands, like the crowd of oppressed, anonymous individual persons who are guilty, indifferent, ashamed.

In the Eucharist, when we are not sitting in the school of discipleship that opens the scriptures to us, we stand before the God who stood with us, who sits in glory. And as we stand we also identify ourselves with all on earth who do not have a chair.

Thought for the day

Upon earth, often enough, to love is to suffer. In heaven to love is to enjoy. (Dom Augustine Morris OSB 1905–1997)

Prayer

Christ, the sun of righteousness,
rise in our hearts this day,
enfold us in the brightness of your love
and bear us at the last to heaven's horizon,
for your love's sake. Amen.

Taming tempters

Is 55:10–11; Ps 34; Mt 6:7–15

> *Jesus said, 'I bless you, Father, Lord of heaven and earth, for hiding these things from the learned and the cleaver and revealing them to mere children.'*
>
> (Matthew 11:25)

Distractions in prayer are commonplace. They flirt with us, if we let them. But they use methods that can also befriend us. Our distractions are often unsuppressed memories, visual recollections and imaginings, a lazily remembered image working upon a mind seeking relief from activity. If we fear and fight them, they've won. If we name the power they use, we can grow confident in prayer and peace of mind.

Some of the most popular and effective ways of dealing with this employ the very media that our distractions use: the memory and the imagination. Pictures, statues, devotional practices, familiar forms of prayer all work for good on these two aspects of our human capacity.

With this positive welcome of the exercise of our memory and imagination this gospel reading from Matthew might prompt us to ask, 'What do you imagine when you pray the Lord's Prayer?' This is not a theoretical question about how prayer works, although it may be connected to that. It is far more a question about how you understand yourself in relation to the words you are using.

So, for example, do you see yourself among the twelve praying with Jesus, or as one of their number without Jesus and having to remember words in which he had previously always led them?

Do you see yourself praying alone or do you remember others who have prayed this prayer with you and whose names inevitably introduce themselves uninvited but welcome?

Does this prayer locate you in a wider community that you can imagine surrounding you unseen? If prayed in an empty church, can you populate the seats with others who go there to pray?

And does this question of what you imagine not also prompt us to ask what God sees when we pray this prayer? At the Lord's Prayer in the great monastery of St Benoit-sur-Loire the whole congregation turns east and extending their hands, like the celebrant of the Eucharist, prays together, 'Notre Père …'

Our prayer, and imagination, must surely be that when we pray this prayer God the Father should see in us the image of Jesus, the beloved who eternally stretches out to the Father in the embrace of the Holy Spirit. When other distractions intersect the imagination with which we might enfold this prayer, we are brought back to our limitations and the sharpness of the Lord's good words: 'Forgive us, them … not into temptation … deliver from evil.'

Thought for the day

The person who prays will have a heart as wide as the love of God itself. (Mother Mary Clare SLG 1906–1988)

Prayer

Send your holy angels to watch over us, O God,
that our prayer may be directed to your glory,
that our hearts may be kindled by your love,
and that we may taste of your goodness
in the land of the living
Through Jesus Christ the Lord. Amen.

Exotic attraction

Jon 3:1–10; Ps 51; Lk 11:29–32

> *It is of the mysterious wisdom of God that we talk, the wisdom that was hidden, which God predestined to be for our glory before the ages began.* (1 Corinthians 2:7)

The Queen of the South is one of my favourite gospel characters.

She represents a rich and sophisticated culture from beyond the Judaeo-Christian tradition. Cast an eye over the account of her visit in 1 Kings 10; Jerusalem was impressed.

The description of her native land at the 'end of the earth' is apt. Sheba is located in the south of the Arabian peninsula, in present day Yemen. In the ancient world the people of this land traded in spices, frankincense, gold, and precious stones. And their Queen was famous, known in Arabic legend as Bilkîs.

In the Old Testament description of the Queen of the South's visit to Solomon the two monarchs represent the aspirations and achievements of their people.

In her wonder at the diet, fashion, culture, and government of Solomon's Jerusalem, the Queen saw a sign of blessing for the people of Israel. The social implications are important here. We ought not to underestimate the significance of the reference Jesus makes to the Queen of the South. But in order to understand it we have to read the text carefully: 'something greater than Solomon is here.'

The reference is not to the person of Jesus, but to a thing; what is it?

Matthew locates this saying between Jesus sending the twelve to proclaim the closeness of the kingdom of Heaven, and Jesus extending the teaching he had given the twelve by his own proclamation of the kingdom to the crowds at the lakeside.

Luke structures the location slightly differently. He places this saying in the context of Jesus turning his face towards Jerusalem, indicating by some stern sayings that the journey to the holy City is symbolic of his vocation to proclaim and reveal the kingdom of God.

The Queen of the South recognised that wisdom is manifest in the quality of a society ordered upon justice. But we know how precarious that can be, as history demonstrates. What Jesus teaches us is the wisdom of love exemplified by the material, spiritual and social fruits of justice and mercy.

Today, it is the developing nations of the world that stand in the place of the Queen of the South as a sign of judgement. If they are to find the authentic Wisdom of God in the gospel of Jesus Christ, it must be through the quality of the civilization of the kingdom of Heaven that his disciples teach, demand and reveal in life and action.

Thought for the day

Wisdom consists in pursuing a worthy God by proper means. (Mary Astell 1668–1731)

Prayer

Lord Jesus Christ,
as we sit at your feet
teach us your living way,
for you are our Word and our Wisdom,
one God with the Father and the Holy Spirit,
now and for ever. Amen.

A casting role

Est 4:1–3, 5:12; Ps 138; Mt 7:7–12

> *In everything we prove ourselves authentic servants of God … poor, yet making many people rich; having nothing, and yet owning everything.*
>
> (2 Corinthians 6:4, 10)

If you were making a film of the story of Esther, who would you cast as this young, delicate, beautiful, devout, and intelligent woman?

I would have invited the following for audition: Ingrid Bergman, for her role as Ilsa in *Casablanca*; Audrey Hepburn, because of the way she played Eliza Doolittle in *My Fair Lady*; and the astonishingly accomplished Scarlett Johansson for Griet, who was *The Girl with a Pearl Earring*. Why?

Ilsa elicits a depth of unacknowledged emotion in Rick Blaine (Humphrey Bogart) a man who struggles for survival in wartime Africa. Eliza Doolittle brings humour and release to the English culture of masculine privilege and social snobbery, shortly before it was dismembered by the First World War. In 17th century Amsterdam the unknown servant who poses for Vermeer inspires a great artist and discredits a rich and lecherous patron by her truer love for Pieter, the butcher's boy.

These characters illustrate the sort of woman that Esther was. They might also help us to see why she belongs so clearly to a tradition that finds its fullest expression in Mary the mother of Jesus.

Here in the New Testament we are presented with another woman whose image has often been claimed as a sign of hope by those enmeshed in self-destructive habits. Mary stands with those who live in a context of oppression – military, political and social, and she exemplifies the innocence and potency of human love.

From Esther and Mary flows a tradition of women who powerfully cast aside the allurement, misuse and pretensions of human power by their clear focus on the eternal truth of God.

In the early Church Perpetua a wealthy young mother and her companion Felicity identify themselves with Jesus in the poverty of death as a statement of the reality of the life beyond death, and through prayer and faith in that life came reconciliation and healing to Perpetua's family and Christian community.

As the Christian era headed towards the close of its second millennium, another woman, Edith Stein – a Jew, a Catholic, a Carmelite nun – was in a similar prison, Auschwitz, revealing the strength of sacrificial love against which the synthetic power of evil could not prevail.

Today Esther, Mary, Perpetua, Felicity, Edith Stein, and all their companions invite us to share with them in that divine wealth that chooses a form of poverty to unmask the spiritually impoverished and morally unbalanced systems of worldly power.

Thought for the day

Our works are the best proofs that the favours we have received come from God. (Teresa of Avila 1515–1582)

Prayer

God, you sent your Son to our world
to bring us home to you;
give us your songs to sing, that even in exile
we may be filled with the breath of your Spirit,
through Jesus the Lord. Amen.

What does greed look like?

Ezk 18:21–28; Ps 130; Mt 5:20–26

> *Alas for you who are rich: you are having your consolation now.*
> *Alas for you who have plenty to eat now: you shall go hungry.*
> *Alas for you who are laughing now: you shall mourn and weep.*
>
> (Luke 6:24–25)

We probably recognise the symptoms quite easily: the overflowing food plate, the drive full of cars, the wardrobe that bulges with unnecessary clothes, shelves of things we simply could not resist.

Greed is superficiality, described in the letter to the Colossians as an earthly thing, 'the same as worshipping a false god.' This suggests that greed in fact looks like a very thin layer; it's a refusal to live with the dangerous possibilities of depth.

Depth takes us into relationships that go beyond the three dimensional aspects of life. In this respect depth shows us the difference between a 'false god', characterised as an idol that is contained within some effigy that you can walk round, measure and quantify, and the God who is beyond all these categories, characterised by an icon, a window into the sense of beyond.

So greed first of all like loneliness in denial. Greed cannot understand the attraction of relatedness to other people. Greed looks at the world as the arena in which other people are the competitive threat to what I have and want, or worse, they are the means by which I acquire it.

But the current of superficiality also drags in its wake the very things that greed desires, and diminishes them. Greed sees everything as objects that are quantifiable. Greed looks like life only ever viewed through the microscope of fact. Greed sees a painting by Cézanne and knows its financial value but not its beauty. Greed assesses a meal by the amount on the plate or the number of Michelin stars awarded to the menu, but fails to appreciate the companionship of the table or the privilege of having food to eat.

Greed is also time limited. It is incapable of perceiving that within the limits of time eternity is to be caught, as 'God's breath in man returning to his birth ... Heaven in ordinarie', in the words of George Herbert. This is where greed looks robotic: superficially human in appearance, but only the sum of its accumulated parts.

When Jesus tells his disciples that their virtue must go deeper than that of the scribes and Pharisees, he is pointing them to a vocation that defies the limitations within which greed flourishes. From that prison you cannot get out, says Jesus, till you have paid the last penny.

Thought for the day

Before you finish eating your breakfast this morning, you've depended on half the world. This is the way our universe is structured. (Martin Luther King 1929–1968)

Prayer

Thirsting on the cross,
you shared the reproach of the oppressed
and carried the sins of all.
May those who despair find you
those who are afflicted rest in you
and the whole creation come to life in you, Amen.

Whose umbrella?

Dt 26:16–19; Ps 119; Mt 5:43–48

> *And when they acknowledged the grace that had been given to me, then James and Cephas and John ... asked nothing more than that we should remember the poor, as indeed I was anxious to do in any case.*
>
> (Galatians 2:9,10)

Imperialism can create an exaggerated view of one's own importance. An example of this distortion is neatly summed up in the ambiguous observation that the English are a self-made people who worship their creator. Perhaps at one stage of our history we did form the impression that God was rather like us: decent, reasonable and Oxbridge.

So a gospel reading that speaks about the weather (a very English preoccupation) is talking our kind of language. The business of the rain falling on honest and dishonest alike was carefully explained to me in the following simple terms: the rain falls more on the honest because the dishonest has got the honest person's umbrella.

These may appear to be flippant comments, but they may also touch a nerve when we ask what it means to be perfect, as our heavenly Father is perfect.

The first challenge to us is to resist the notion that God is somehow a projection of our better, greater selves; perfection in others is then assessed by the extent to which they attain the standard of goodness we ourselves have set.

However, seeking to be perfect, like God, demands something more profoundly disturbing. It suggests that we consult not our comfortable groupings of the like-minded, but people very different from us who can teach us something about the extent to which we are, as yet, very different from God.

When looking for such teachers we ought always to inquire of the poor, those who speak an international language of loss, within which they also hold the capacity for generosity, joy and patience. Here we might find ourselves in an uncomfortable position, sheltering from the rain beneath the honest person's umbrella.

For when we from the privileged world face the rest of the world's population, we have to admit that the gifts of God given for all in creation have accrued to just a few of us in quite unmistakable ways: education, housing, the arts, entertainment and recreation, medical care, trade systems – to name a few.

And living among the poor we may find that the compelling examples of the perfection of God come from those who are our equivalent of 'tax collectors and pagans', i.e. not like us. These are the professional people who may not claim to love God but who, for love of the poor, live a life of self-sacrifice that comes as close as any to the perfection sought by the disciples of Jesus Christ.

Thought for the day

Overcoming poverty is not a gesture of charity. It is an act of justice. (Nelson Mandela b. 1918)

Prayer

In the darkness of unknowing,
when your love seems absent,
draw near to us, O God,
in Christ poor and forsaken,
in Christ risen and glorified,
our redeemer and our Lord. Amen.

Nicholas King SJ

Second Week of Lent

Second Sunday of Lent

God is present where God cannot possibly be

Gn 22: 1–2, 9–13, 15–18; Ps 116; Rm 8:31–34; Mk 9: 2–10

Who will separate us from the love of Christ?
(Romans 8:35)

Those who have the privilege of working with the poorest of the poor know that extraordinary moment, when they find themselves in a situation where they think that God cannot possibly be; and just there, quite suddenly and unexpectedly, they are touched by the presence of the Spirit of God. To be in South Africa in the days of apartheid, and in the years when the evil of apartheid was finally being driven out, was to experience precisely such a moment.

Like many of you who are making this Lenten journey, I have known the touch of that presence at an AIDS deathbed, in a prison for sex-offenders, and serving the sick in Lourdes. Today's readings speak of the God who is in such impossible places.

The first reading is the most chilling story in the whole Old Testament, when Abraham would have killed his beloved son; we notice that Isaac never says a word to his father again, and that Sarah dies immediately after this episode, so it is a horror story; and yet God was there, bringing peace out of the disaster.

The psalm knows that God is there when things are at their worst. 'I trusted, even when I said "I am sorely afflicted"' the poet sings; but as always in Israel's praying, even when their lamentations are loudest, there is great hope: 'you have loosened my bonds'.

The second reading is the wonderfully poetic climax of Paul's statement of the Christians' grounds for hope, one of those purple passages that enable us to forgive Paul all his crustiness. This is a song to sing in dark places where God seems to be absent.

Today's gospel, the story of the Transfiguration, comes immediately after the dark shadow of the cross has for the first time fallen over Mark's gospel. The Church always reads this story to itself on this second Sunday in Lent, to offer a glimpse of the Resurrection, so far ahead in the future, and so impossibly unimaginable in the mess that is our world. As Elijah and Moses talk to Jesus, and God affirms that Jesus is indeed his Son, and therefore death will not be the end of his story, we take hope as we look at the headlines in today's newspapers.

Thought for the day

Where the darkness is most menacing, God is discreetly but powerfully there.

Prayer

Lord, help us on our Lenten journey,
teach us that you are with us on the road, especially when it is hard.
Teach us above all that you are there, most of all, and however bad it may be,
in those who suffer and those who have nothing.
Teach us to stretch out our hands to them, and so find you. Amen.

God's generosity, and the mess we make of it

Dn 9: 4–10; Ps 79: 8–9, 11, 13; Lk 6: 36–38

Let your compassion hasten to meet us. (Psalm 79:8)

CAFOD and Christian Aid only exist because of the mess we have made of our world, and because God's unfailing generosity always brings a compassionate response out of human beings. Again and again in South Africa it was the case that the poorest of the poor showed astonishing generosity, giving of what they did not have to those who had even less, and making the world a better place.

Today's first reading is an attempt to grapple with the grim realities of history: Jerusalem occupied and destroyed by a hostile power, and the people scattered. We begin to cope with the disaster when we recognise the mess we have made: 'we have sinned, we have done wrong, we have acted wickedly, we have betrayed your commandments and your ordinances, and we have turned away from them'. Our comfortable life in the West comes at a price that is paid by others; and we need God's help to put things right.

The psalm recognises our failures, but also asserts God's overflowing determination to make good what has gone wrong. 'Do not treat us according to our sins, O Lord', we beg . . . 'O Lord our God, forgive us our sins; rescue us for the sake of your name'.

And that is the message of today's gospel: 'be compassionate as your Father is compassionate'. Why? This is because generosity is the 'name of the game'; generosity is the principle on which the universe is constructed; generosity is who God is. And this generosity is given wonderful expression in a very striking image: 'a good measure, pressed down, shaken up and overflowing, will be poured into your lap', Jesus confidently proclaims. The difficulty is that we don't really believe that if we give 'there will be gifts'; with our dreary mathematics we foolishly think that the more we give the less we have. Let us today respond with the generosity that is at the very heart of who we are.

Thought for the day

It is more blessed to give than to receive.

Prayer

God our generous Father,
your generosity is beyond anything that we can imagine.
Give us the grace today not to run from it,
but to embrace it with love.
May your generosity radiate from us to all the world.
Amen.

A shock to our complacency

Is 1:10, 16–20; Ps 50:8–9, 16–17, 21, 23; Mt 23:1–18

"Don't call anyone on earth 'Father'!"

We have a dangerous ability to erect walls of complacency, in order to defend ourselves against God's challenge. All of us human beings are, whatever the appearances we seek to maintain, desperately insecure; now we can in fact find our security only in God, but we tell ourselves that if only we can make our bank balance big enough, or sufficiently fill our larders and cellars, or install the latest and best in burglar alarms, or go loyally to church on Sundays, then we shall find the security we are looking for. Wrong.

And so in the well-fed West we can rehearse our shabby reasons why people in Africa should be starving – until God brings us face to face with what that means. In today's first reading, Isaiah is in fiery mood, attacking the religious leaders of his time (that's you and me, in case you find yourself purring in agreement with the prophet) as 'rulers of Sodom ... people of Gomorrah', precisely because they were religious but unloving.

The psalm does the same, for those who take ritual seriously but ignore the commandments of God. 'I do not ask more bullocks from your farms', God bellows at us, as we try to find an excuse for our indifference to others.

And the gospel? The gospel should make us shiver in our shoes – for it is not addressed to religious leaders of long ago, but to us, any of us who hide behind our religious sensibility, and quietly insist on maintaining our own status, instead of acknowledging the

Fatherhood of God. It is we who too readily defend our own tendency to 'tie up heavy burdens and lay them on people's shoulders' without offering to alleviate them. Let us pray today to become instead the servants of our brothers and sisters. If we can contemplate with equanimity the fact that our fellow-humans are in need while we are comfortably off, then we have not begun to understand what it means to call God 'our Father'.

Thought for the day

The Pharisees were 'good religious people'.

Prayer

Dear Lord, we have many ways of avoiding your call.
Teach us, with your gentle challenge,
not to wriggle our evasions,
but to embrace you as Father,
And everyone else as sister and brother.
Then teach us how to live that in our lives. Amen.

Persecution or power?

Jr 18:18–10; Ps 31:5–6; Mt 20:17–28

> *'The Son of Man will be handed over … to mock, and flog, and crucify'* (Matthew 20: 28–19)

When working in Africa, I always felt a queasy spasm whenever I heard of church leaders demanding that the government should pay them more attention, take them more seriously, or boasting of their intimacy with the secular authorities. That is not what Christianity is about, even though down the millennia, it has been a standing temptation for Christians to leap into bed with the powerful. Today's readings remind us that if we are to be serious about our discipleship, we must expect persecution; so if we are too popular with the authorities, we might need to ask what we are doing wrong. That might be a useful thought to take with us through the rest of Lent.

Jeremiah is complaining to God about the plots against his life: 'Come on – let us concoct a plot against Jeremiah; the priest will not run short of instruction without him'; but it does not have much effect. 'Who needs Jeremiah?' is the question on the lips of his religiously-minded contemporaries, and Jeremiah is not at all sure that God is on his side.

The psalmist is solidly determined to trust in God, even as he faces 'terror all around me'. Characteristically, the poet is more optimistic than Jeremiah, 'I trust in you, Lord, I say "You are my God".' But he is well aware that being a believer does not mean that everyone will admire you. Rather the contrary.

And in the gospel, when Jesus explains to his somewhat dim-witted disciples that their leader has to die, they don't take a blind bit of notice. Instead, two of them set up their mother to get the top posts for them ('promise that these two sons of mine may sit one at your right hand and the other at your left in your kingdom'), while all the rest get cross at this power-play, fearful that they will be cheated out of their rightful status. Our invitation is not to climb the greasy pole of church (or other) politics, but to follow Jesus, whatever the cost.

Thought for the day

God's power is fragile and vulnerable.

Prayer

Lord, in our insecurity, we often feel that life would be better
if we were among the rulers of the earth.
Teach us that our only security lies in you
and that persecution doesn't mean that we have got it wrong.
Teach us to be like you in all that we do. Amen.

A tree planted near streams of water

Jr 17: 5–10; Ps 1: 1–4, 6; Lk 16: 19–31

> *Lazarus was carried by the angels into the bosom of Abraham.* (Luke 16: 22)

Today's readings invite us to make our Lenten choice, between life and death. That, of course, is not a choice that is available to a significant proportion of the world's population, especially in sub-Saharan Africa. They are surrounded by death, partly because of the life-destructive choices that we have made in the affluent West.

The first reading and the psalm use an image that strikes powerfully home in the dry climates of Africa and the Near East: listening to God, and doing what God wants, is the equivalent for us of a tree being planted near a river. Both Jeremiah and the psalmist challenge us to put out roots into the life that comes from God; our danger, and Lent is perhaps a time for us to become aware of the menace, is that we shall unthinkingly postpone such (literally) radical measures until we are comfortably off.

But everyone in those parts knows what a tree without access to water looks like – dry and dead, and easily blown away. And that is what poet and prophet challenge us with today. What are we to do in order to choose life?

Challengingly and dramatically the gospel tells us: pay attention to the poor at your gates. Lazarus (whose name means 'God has helped') is of almost no significance in the story, except that he moves automatically into life ('the bosom of Abraham'). This profoundly subversive story starts with the eye-catching description of the anonymous rich man and his consumerist life-style. 'There was a rich man who used to dress in purple and fine linen and feast magnificently every day.' This is followed by the alarming contrast: 'a poor man ... covered with sores, who longed to fill himself with the scraps that fell from the rich man's table. Dogs even came and licked his sores.' Where do you fit into this story?

Thought for the day

You can, today, choose between life and death.

Prayer

God our Creator,
you will us into life, feed us and water us.
Teach us to answer your generosity with a generosity of
our own.
Teach us to be attentive to the poor in our streets.
Teach us to choose, not Death, but Life,
with your Son, Our Lord Jesus Christ. Amen.

God's fidelity even through death

Gn 37: 3–4, 12–13, 17–28; Ps 105; 16–21; Mt 21: 33–43, 45– 46

> *'They took him, and flung him out of the vineyard, and killed him.'* (Matthew 21: 39)

There is murder about in today's readings. Murder seems an obvious solution once you lose sight of God's faithfulness, and forget that God does not have favourites; and those who have committed murder will tell you how obvious and natural a solution it can seem, if God is not part of the equation.

Joseph's brothers, irritated by his tactless dreams and their father's blatant favouritism for the youngster, fling him into a well. They even calmly hold a banquet while he is imprisoned – and they have no intention that he should ever emerge from his place of incarceration. But God is in charge, and we are only at the beginning of the Joseph story, a long way from its triumphant ending.

This is what the psalmist proclaims as he meditates on Joseph's escape – and it was God's doing, when 'the king sent and released him; the ruler of the peoples set him free'.

Today's gospel is part of a series of angry confrontations between Jesus and his religious opponents at this point in Matthew's gospel, the upshot of his provocative and prophetic gesture of 'cleansing the Temple'. It is clearly an account of Israel's murderous infidelity, as Matthew indicates with his unmistakeable reference to Isaiah's 'Song of the Vineyard', which was all about Israel's infidelity. That realisation does not, however, mean that we can breathe a sigh of relief and condemn those whom Jesus is attacking. This gospel challenges us, demands of us that we reflect where and when we have similarly chased off the servants of the landowner and expelled and killed the son. Lent is not, you see, for our comfort.

But God will remain faithful; God's purposes cannot be defeated. And what about our infidelity? Will later generations, and, more significantly, God, charge us with murder, for our indifference to the starving, or for our greedy destruction of the planet?

Thought for the day

Joseph's dreams nearly had him killed; and God used his dreams to get him freed.

Prayer

Faithful and loving Lord,
may your fidelity overcome our murderous hatreds,
may your love prove victorious over our destructive egoism;
and may we build a kingdom of justice, love and peace.
Amen.

God's challenging compassion

Mi 7:14–15, 18–20; Ps 103:1–4, 9-12; Lk 15:1–3, 11–32

'His father ... ran and fell on his neck, and kissed him!' (Luke 15:20)

Compassionate is a difficult quality to handle. On the one hand we find it hard to exercise compassion towards those who are different from us: sometimes we find ourselves muttering 'Why are they so irresponsible? Why don't they go out and get a job?' Sometimes we lapse into a kind of condescending pity, and buy *The Big Issue* or send a cheque to CAFOD, which may make us feel better, but may have nothing to do with the compassion of God, nor with building God's kingdom. Today's readings speak to us of this compassionate God of ours, who 'will hurl all our sins into the depths of the sea', in the words of the poem with which the Micah scroll ends. Micah insists that this God pays careful attention to 'the flock that is your heritage', and that we need God to 'read down our faults'.

That compassion, however, which the psalmist also celebrates, with his cheerful affirmation of God's blessings (my soul, give thanks to the Lord'), and his affirmation that God is 'the one who forgives all your iniquity ... God has distanced our transgressions from us'), does not mean that God is 'easy'.

Look at today's gospel, and the pain that the Pharisees felt when they saw Jesus' undesirable friends. In reply Jesus tells the story of a father and his two undesirable sons. The younger of the two virtually sentences his father to death ('give me the money – now') and then runs home when his recipe for a 'good time' doesn't work. The older sulks like mad at the father's compassionate generosity. The father treats them both the same, and gently waits for their response to his love.

Neither of them can cope with their father's love. Luke does not tell us whether the elder son joins the party. That is because it depends on you, the reader. How will you respond to God's challenging compassion?

Thought for the day

Better to be relieved by God's poor taste in friends than to be shocked by it.

Prayer

God our Prodigal Father,
your compassion sometimes upsets us.
Your running to embrace us is a bit of an embarrassment
to us.
Teach us to know our need of your love;
teach us to accept it happily into our lives. Amen.

Kathy Galloway

Third week of Lent

Third Sunday of Lent

Outside holiness

Ex 20:1–17; Ps 19; 1 Cor 1:22–25; Jn 2:13–25

'Stop making my father's house a market-place!'
(John 2:16)

In Jesus' Jerusalem, being considered a sinner was a lot to do with being poor. According to the teachings of the law, there were certain requirements that people had to fulfil, and many of these had to do with making the right kind of sacrifices in the temple. Some were monetary, some were small animals or birds which would be killed and offered; but even these had to be purchased from the market traders. A brisk business went on, right inside the temple.

But a great many people were very poor, and had either to borrow the money to buy the offerings, or couldn't afford them at all. If you borrowed, you weren't in a position to bargain – you just had to take the rate the moneylenders offered. And you stood a good chance of being fleeced. So if you were poor, you had the choice – either get into debt to fulfil your obligations, or default on them, and find yourself classified among the sinners, and thus excluded. You didn't have to do anything we might consider morally wrong to be a sinner, you just had to be poor.

This was a fairly brutal kind of commodification – it turned people's devotion into something that was bought and sold. In so doing, it also commodified their whole belonging and identity within the community. It made a mockery of the justice and faithfulness of God. It put huge numbers of people outside holiness. And this exploitation enraged Jesus, happening as it did right inside the house of God. His action in overturning the moneylenders was a great shout of outrage.

Jesus turned the tables when the love of God, which is a free gift, was turned into a commercial transaction which oppressed the poor. Still today, the free gifts of God, those things necessary to sustain life, are turned into commercial transactions which oppress the poor. Land, oceans, rivers, the water we drink, even the very air we breathe are bought, sold and used in ways that exclude and damage the poorest communities on earth. Sometimes it is even suggested that this is given divine sanction. Not by Jesus!

Thought for the Day

Do *our* economics put people outside holiness?

Prayer

God, forgive us if we profit from the suffering of others
Remind us that we have power in our choices
if we act together.
Lead us to choose justice,
in our politics, in our economics, in our churches.
Justice, beginning where we are ... Amen.

'I kent his faither...'

2 K 5: 1-15; Ps 42-43; Lk 4: 24-30

They said, 'Isn't he the son of Joseph?' (Luke 4:24)

Jesus also knew what it was like to be considered outside holiness. There is an old saying in Scotland: 'Him ... I kent his faither' (I knew his father). It's used as a put-down, when it's thought that someone is getting above his station, and it's a good way of being able to then ignore what that person is saying, especially if it's uncomfortable or challenging. There is something of this in Jesus' recognition that 'no prophet is accepted in the prophet's home town'. As long as he was doing and saying things that reflected well on them, Jesus' townsfolk in Nazareth were very happy to accept him ('isn't that Joseph's son?'). But when he began to say things they didn't want to hear, things that might disturb the status quo, they turned against him, ran him out of town and would have lynched him, except that his personal authority allowed him to go free of them.

And his offence? Only to remind them that the prophet Elijah had been given food and shelter in a time of famine by a widow in Sidon, and that the prophet Elisha, at a time when there were many lepers in Israel, had healed only Naaman the Syrian. And that both the widow and Namaan were not Jews, were outside the covenant, and yet their faithfulness and obedience had been exemplary, and had made the power of God visible.

It's always a challenge to accept this fundamental teaching of Jesus that the love of God and the power of God extends far beyond those who are like us, those whom we like, those who think or believe or worship like us. God is active also in and through the 'other' – the stranger, the foreigner, those we think of as the enemy, those we think of as outside holiness. But Jesus frequently pointed to those 'outside holiness' as demonstrating some facet of the divine life, and was himself happy to serve them, to receive from them, and to share food and friendship and learning with them.

Thought for the Day
In Jesus, there is nowhere and no one 'outside holiness.'

Prayer
Lord Jesus, I am too often scandalized by who you love.
Help me to see that the failure of judgement,
of imagination,
of compassion,
is mine, not yours.
Help me to see the other with your eyes. Amen

A different way of seeing

Dn 3:25, 34–43; Ps 25; Mt 18:21–35

> *'The king felt sorry for him, so he forgave him the debt ...'* (Matthew 18:27)

Here is a rich and profound text from Matthew's gospel. Peter asks Jesus how often he must forgive a wrong against him. To illustrate the nature of forgiveness, Jesus tells the story of two men who both owed money, who had debts they could not pay. One was a little debt, one was a huge debt. One was forgiven, the other was not.

It would be a mistake to draw too close a parallel from this story of debt cancellation. The International Monetary Fund and the World Bank bear little resemblance to the moneylender, still less are they like the forgiving God of whom Jesus talks. And the cancellation of debt is not to be simply equated with the forgiveness of sins – in any case, today, the weight of injustice is tilted in the other direction, for the debt burden of the poorest countries is huge, unfair and the capital has been repaid many times over.

Nevertheless, there is a deep truth here that has some relevance – about the attitude of the heart, the hardness which causes partial vision. We see our own self-righteousness, or self-interest, and it narrows our horizons, blinds us to another kind of reality. The king saw the man who owed him much with the eyes of compassion; it was a new way of seeing, and it opened up many possibilities, including the possibility of forgiveness and generosity.

That melting of the hardened heart is the experience of grace, which comes when we are vulnerable, exposed, personal, not self-justifying. It expresses itself freely and extravagantly. If freedom is the ability to look another straight in the eye, unbound, then grace is a new way of seeing, with the eyes of compassion, which transforms our reality.

If we have anything different as Christians to bring to our life and work, it is surely this experience of grace, unconditional in its giving and receiving, as the context and reality, as the wider vision against which we measure our principles *and* our practice. It is this experience which binds us together in the community of those who see each other with the eyes of love.

Thought for the Day

Forgiveness is never just a thought or a feeling. It is always an action.

Prayer

Generous God,
Never let me forget the grace by which I live,
but unlock my heedless heart
and open it to compassion
and uncalculating love. Amen.

At the heart of the Law

Dt 4: 1, 5-9; Ps 147; Mt 5: 17-19

'I have come to make their teachings come true.'
(Matthew 5:17)

All of this week's lectionary gospel readings have in common that in them, Jesus reflects on the nature of the Law, that Law which was at the heart of what it meant to be a Jew. And at the heart of the Law was the relationship with God. In part, Jesus is saying what the Law is not.

It is not a series of propositions to which one gives intellectual assent.

It is not a theory, it is a practice. It needs to be applied to have life.

It is not a guarantee of special favour or privileged treatment to the people of the covenant.

It is not a means to exclude those of other communities or beliefs.

It is not a stick with which to beat those who are most vulnerable.

It is not something that can be narrowly applied only when it is in one's interest and disregarded when it is not.

It is not something to be worshipped in and for itself, but rather understood as that which will lead people more closely into solidarity with the divine purpose.

When he was asked what he thought of Christianity, Gandhi famously said that he thought it was a very good thing, and more Christians should practice it! In his teaching, through parable, story, demonstration, action, Jesus keeps bringing his enquirers and inquisitors back to what the Law is for. Far from disregarding it, or bringing it into disrepute, as his detractors wanted to prove he was doing, he is actually confronting them with its desirability, its need for accomplishment. But that, as Paul was later to point out, meant living in its spirit of justice and mercy, not just paying lip-service to its letter.

This passage comes in the Sermon on the Mount, just after the Beatitudes, in which Jesus speaks of the struggle to love and the paradox of fulfilment. Sorrow, humility, the hunger for right relationship, compassion, integrity, peacemaking, persecution, above all, the knowledge of the need of God; *these* are the characteristics of faithfulness to the Law and the prophets.

Thought for the Day

Our faith only becomes real when we practice it.

Prayer

Lord Jesus,
Lead me in my life and witness
so that I may follow you
into a closer relationship with God. Amen

Living in one world

Jr 7: 23–28; Ps 95; Lk 11:14–23

> *'... a family divided against itself falls apart.'*
>
> (Luke 11:17)

'A house divided against itself cannot stand.' So said Jesus, and the household of humanity is always illustrating this truth. When all the members of a household are at odds with one another, when they fear and suspect each other, then the life of the household is unhappy, tense, and full of threat. One option is for the strongest people in the house simply to expel those who they don't like or agree with. But that doesn't really solve anything. The word 'sectarian' comes from the Latin word meaning 'to cut', and that's what sectarianism does – it cuts up the household, and it actually makes everyone weaker.

This tendency to separate, polarise and set in opposition encourages us to live in the illusion that somehow we can draw imaginary boundaries within which we are protected, can operate with impunity, can act without consequences. In the private, illusory world of our individual or collective wilfulness, we can pretend that life can be lived without consequences – no hurt children, no African countries devastated by the arms trade, no global warming – or we can spin the consequences so that they become the fault of those in the alternative worlds. So we accommodate our consciences to our desires.

But in the process, we become less than whole. We learn to live in a climate of mistrust, suspicion and betrayal, not just of those outwith our illusory worlds, but of those within them too. We create cultures characterised by secrecy, shame and fear of transparency, for these are the walls which protect our worlds. We learn to have many faces. This is the way that abuse happens.

And it is an abuse of power above all. Those who are the poorest and most vulnerable do not have the luxury, because they do not have the power, of creating alternative worlds in which there are no consequences. They just have to live in the dangerous, violent, precarious, threatened and globalised planet Earth, bearing everyone else's externalised consequences. If spirituality is to have any meaning, surely it must be about how we live together in this one fragile real world.

Thought for the day

Someone, somewhere, bears the consequences of our actions, for good or for ill

Prayer

O Christ,
strengthen us to resist the false attraction of easy answers,
magic fixes,
abuses of power,
and the delusion that there is any way apart from justice
in which God's justice can be done. Amen

Life before death

Ho 14: 2–10; Ps 81, Mk 12: 8–34

'God is God not of the dead but of the living.'
(Mark 12:27)

Christian Aid has as its slogan, 'We believe in life before death.' I am reminded of it when I read today's passage, in which Jesus is once again being questioned, this time by the Sadducees, who want to know about the marital arrangements in heaven. This is another legalistic question; Jesus' frustration with their scrupulosity is evident. They are asking the wrong questions, trying to make the framework of one way of being fit a quite different reality. He is not going to answer questions about death, because 'God is God not of the dead but of the living.' Christian Aid, like CAFOD, is concerned with the well-being of the living; not because life before death is the whole story, but because that is the life that humankind has been given responsibility to care for.

Last year, the Iona Community responded to a request to send one of our members to accompany a church in Gugulethu, South Africa, which has a dedicated ministry among people living with HIV/AIDS. His purpose was to immerse himself in the challenge of the devastation of AIDS in the midst of poverty, to share the burden of understanding God's presence there, and to make theology anew around it in reflection and story.

We accepted this invitation to accompaniment, and to wrestling with the question, 'In the midst of so much suffering and death, what does it mean to affirm *life*?' We knew that in order to approach this task with integrity, it was a question we would have to ask ourselves, not just in a South African context but in our own lives.

We learned from, and were humbled by, the courage, faith and cheerfulness of people living with HIV/AIDS. We reaffirmed the importance of accompaniment, walking with people, being alongside them, sometimes when there is nothing we can do to 'fix' things. We were reminded, because we saw it daily in action, of the commandment to love our neighbours as we love ourselves. Sometimes, often, that's simply about showing up and saying 'yes' to life, and no to all that denies life.

Thought for the Day

God is in the township – both weeping and dancing with the people.

Prayer

Though I am poor, God is with me in the morning when I wake up:
God is around during sleep, and is with me as I try to walk around.
I just cry knowing that God has heard my prayer.
I live with great hope. Amen.

(*From a prayer from Gugulethu, translated from Xhosa*)

Denying our need

Ho 5:15–6: 6; Ps 51; Lk 18:9–14

> *'I thank you ... that I am not like ... everybody else.'*
> (Luke 18:11)

We who are Christians are invited to trust the fact that we have intrinsic worth. We are family, made in the image of God. And because we are loved, we can be forgiven, healed, held, set free, we can grow. To know our intrinsic worth to God, that in spite of all we do we are of infinite value, is to be saved. But if we are family, we are not only children. I am not the only loved one. Grace is not just mine. Who is my brother? Who is my sister? These relationships go far beyond kinship, nationality, race, religion, politics. If I would call God father, then the tax-collector is my brother.

This story has overtones of the 'good elder brother' and the 'bad younger brother' in the story of the lost son earlier in Luke's gospel. They're family values stories read from a different perspective. And we all have self-righteous, elder brother, Pharisee parts of ourselves. But when family values are extended beyond our front door, or beyond our church walls, or beyond our national borders, questions of morality take on a somewhat different perspective. It's not that right ceases to be right, or wrong ceases to be wrong, it's more that we cease to be so innocent.

Jesus said, the measure you use for others is the measure God will use for you. By the family values of the gospels, our catastrophic economic order, which condemns so many to unremitting poverty but by which we profit, doesn't look very family-friendly. We're all a little tarnished. We're all under judgement. In the family values of the gospels, morality is viewed through the eyes of love, not love through the eyes of morality. Perhaps the real point to this story is not that the Pharisee is more virtuous – there is less difference between us all than we mostly acknowledge – but that his self-righteousness made him proud and self-sufficient. In denying his similarity, he also closed the door to his own need, to the mutuality that is both blessing and responsibility, and to the God who desires to meet our deepest need.

Thought for the day

Recognition of our own frailty is not a threat but a promise.

Prayer

Preserve us from the self-righteousness that makes us
  arrogant,
give us insight to see the structures of injustice by which
  we profit,
and grace to cherish all people in our vulnerability,
knowing that we all live within your love. Amen

Bede Leach OSB

Fourth week of Lent

Fourth Sunday of Lent

The key to making the impossible possible

2 Ch 36:14–16, 19–23; Ps 137; Ep 2:4–10; Jn 3:14–21

> *'At last the wrath of the Lord rose so high against his people that there was no further remedy.'*
>
> (2 Chronicles 36:16)

'They ridiculed the messengers of God, despised his words, laughed at his prophets ... until there was no further remedy.'

We too try the Lord's patience up to and beyond breaking point. The words and actions of our society and its wider world flood in like a spring tide, breaching our feeble, tired defences, overwhelming us, destroying all we have accrued to date.

In Lent, especially, we find ourselves emotionally and spiritually deported, carried off into exile, serving false gods in all their many guises, with little if anything to show for all our efforts. Only then does the Lord intervene. 'He roused the spirit of Cyrus king of Persia', commissioning a pagan king to speak out for, and send back, the chosen people to the promised land.

God acts through the most unlikely people in the most unexpected moments. Why? Because 'God loved the world so much'; so much, costing not less than everything, even the cost of his own Son's life, and not just to save a chosen remnant, but the whole world. 'So that everyone who believes in him may not be lost'; everyone, subject to only one condition – that we believe in him.

And you and I? What will be *our* response? Will it be 'perhaps' or 'as long as' or 'maybe' or will it be a simple, 'Yes, Lord.' If we believe, then everything is possible; we have Our Lord's word for it. The key to making the impossible possible is to believe in it.

Thought for the day

God loved the world so much that he gave his only Son.

Prayer

Father, let the light of your truth
guide us to your kingdom
through a world filled with lights contrary to your own.
May your love make us what you have called us to believe.
We ask this through Christ our Lord. Amen.

A defining moment

Is 65:17–21; Ps 30; Jn 4:43–54

> *'The past will not be remembered, and will come no more to mind.*
> *Rather be joyful, be glad for ever at what I am creating.'*
>
> (Isaiah 65:17–18)

Yesterday, mid-Lent Sunday, was a defining moment, a day to step forward. We can become experts in hindsight, at looking back with regret and self-recrimination. Yet in today's reading Isaiah relays the divine invitation to begin again ... *today*. He proclaims this to be a moment for joy, gladness, and affirmation, not regret, weeping, accusations or self-pity.

How do the people of Zimbabwe listen to, and translate into their lives, these words of divine assurance and promise: 'Never again will there be an infant who lives only a few days'? Then why does my baby die through lack of food or clean water? Why do you, our God, allow such a tragedy if you say you are creating a joyful Jerusalem and a glad people?

It is the same dilemma each and every one of us faces. How can we come to terms with the mystery of suffering? In the gospel, Jesus tests the motivation of the court official whose son was ill. Do you want a lifelong relationship with me, or do you want signs, proofs and an instant cure? he seems to be asking. Is it new life you want or a quick fix?

'Sir, come down before my child dies,' the man replies. He is desperate for the presence of the person of

Jesus. The mystery deepens when Jesus sends him away: 'Go home, your son will live.' Has he been dismissed, rejected, or palmed off?

We tend to seek an explanation, rather than to trust and believe, and the sacrament of the present moment is lost. We are masters of the lost opportunity. Today is a defining moment. It is the time to begin our journey home, not loaded up with reasons and explanations, but aware in faith that, in the company of Jesus, we will discover both the cure and the answer.

Thought for the day

It is the one who responds in faith who discovers the cure.

Prayer

Come, Lord Jesus, walk with us on our journey home,
help us to see you in all who suffer illness, disability or disease.
We make this and all our prayers through Christ our Lord. Amen.

Fruit-bearing and flavourful

Ezk 47:1–9,12; Ps 46; Jn 5:1–3, 5–16

> *'He held his measuring line and measured off a thousand cubits.'* (Ezekiel 47:3)

The angel with his measuring line reminds us of the pace of Lent and the way we grow in faith and self-knowledge week by week: self-appraised, measured, deepening. In a relationship with the divine, the waters of grace emerge initially as a trickle but may eventually grow into a life-giving torrent, enriching all who come into contact with us, within our faith community and beyond. We are capable of becoming fruit-bearing and flavourful, giving taste to what has become ordinary and routine, healing that which has become 'dis-eased'.

Who have you given flavour to so far this week? What sourness or bitterness have you been able to dilute or sweeten, at home, in your parish, in your office or place of work?

In the gospel story of the cure at the Pool of Bethesda, the sick man's cross was three-fold. He had to wait patiently for the life-giving moment of disturbance, yet he could not shake off the realisation that he would never reach the pool in time. Which gave him the most pain? His physical disability? His inability to reach the water in time? Or to seem destined to always come second ('someone else gets there before me')?

Perhaps our fear is that on our journey towards the kingdom there will be moments of disturbance, an opportunity to step out from our paralysis, but we too will be unable to find a neighbour to put us into the pool.

Take heart. 'There is headroom in the cave of Bethlehem for all who know how to stoop' (Ronald Knox). There is a place in the kingdom for all who know how to respond to the voice of the divine helper: 'Get up, pick up your sleeping mat and walk' (John 5:8).

Thought for the day

You have a vocation, a calling: to be a gardener or a pool attendant. The soil and the water challenge us to step out from the pew and from our paralysis. Are you listening?

Prayer

God, Father of all and source of true peace,
help us to live in peace and harmony,
ever alert to your presence and your need
in those paralysed through illness or fear. Amen.

Our calling

Is 49:8–15; Ps 145; Jn 5:17–30

> *'At the favourable time I will answer you, on the day of salvation I will help you.'* (Isaiah 49:8)

Today's first reading opens with a wonderful statement of restoration, of being heard, listened to, and being valued again. We are reminded of our priceless relationship with and in the divine: 'I have formed you and have appointed you.'

'You …' Not the person next to you, but *you*.

A treasured relationship, but one that has perhaps been broken – whether by design or default, accident or mistake. We are left feeling isolated, alone, vulnerable. Is this an image of your Lent, or, more painfully, of much of your journey in life so far? Do you feel you are surviving rather than living, locked in an invisible prison? If so, the voice of the divine whispers to you now. 'Come out … show yourself' (Isaiah 49:9). Emerge from the shadows of guilt and anxiety. Let your real self re-emerge. You are known, recognised, remembered by name: 'I will never forget you. Look, I have engraved you on the palms of my hand' (Isaiah 49:15–16).

In the gospel, Jesus tells us that the favourable time is coming, 'indeed, it is already here' (John 4:25). For John, it is the last times; for some, this is a day to live in fear of, a day of judgement; for others, it is a day of favour and of promise: 'Today you will be with me in paradise.'

Jesus says, 'Whoever listens to my words, and believes in the one who sent me, has eternal life' (John 5:24). These are not words of threat, of prescription or judgement, but of promise. Our calling is to see and to make present paradise on earth, truth and reality, realised and set free, through our prayer and our work for justice. 'Come out ... show yourself.'

Thought for the day

'Come out ...' Find the door to your cell, grasp the handle, and discover it is no longer locked.

Prayer

Father, be with all who are in relationships which threaten and impose
rather than enable and empower.
May your Spirit of truth guide both victim and aggressor
into the freedom of your love and presence. Amen.

A great nation

Ex 32:7–14; Ps 106; Jn 5:31–47

> *Yahweh said to Moses, 'Go down now, because your people whom you brought out of Egypt have apostasised'.* (Exodus 32:7)

They were a people who, with faith and courage, at every cost to themselves and their families, had left Egypt and journeyed into the desert, into the unknown. The reality had proved to be far worse than they had imagined. Lack of food, loss of livelihood and home, constantly on the move and directionless. There was a cloud and a pillar of fire to steer by but the God who had called them to begin was absent. And so they began to ask, 'Where is our God?'

Instead of trying to listen to them and understand them, the God of the Exodus briskly labels them. 'I know these people. I know how headstrong they are.' God threatens them with blazing wrath, whilst, in contrast, the loyal and the dutiful, the law-keepers, are to be rewarded. 'I shall make a great nation out of you instead', he tells Moses.

It seems a theology of division, of disunity; of 'us and them'. But Moses the law-giver steps out beyond the Law, beyond his narrow remit, with its prescriptions and regulations. He speaks up for the excluded, for the disillusioned and the headstrong, and at the same time saves God's reputation. 'Lord, relent, remember your oath and promise.' Why confirm the Egyptians' worst fears about you?

And the Lord relents. He still relents. He listens to

those who speak out for the excluded and the marginalized. He waits longingly and lovingly for our return to him, as we seek to plead, to seek, to thank, to share, on behalf of others.

We can become 'a great nation' not for what we have taken or conquered, but for the generosity with which we share. No 'them', just 'us', everyone needed and included.

Thought for the day

Whilst we fear the prospect of the withering look, the book of judgement, the cane and the fires of hell, the Lord waits with growing excitement and expectation, with our slippers ready and our usual place set at the meal table.

Prayer

Father, your Word, Jesus Christ, spoke peace to a sinful world.
Teach us, who bear his name, to follow his example
in turning hatred to love, conflict to peace, death to eternal life.
We ask this through Christ our Lord. Amen.

The sacrament of the present moment

Ws 2:1,12–22; Ps 34; Jn 7:1–2, 10, 25-30

> *'Let us lie in wait for the virtuous man, since he annoys us ... In his opinion, we are counterfeit.'*
>
> (Wisdom 2:12,16).

In a conflict, there is fault and responsibility on both sides. Who do we annoy or disturb with our piety and religious practice? Someone in our own family? Or a friend? Do they think of us as 'holy Joes' (or 'holy Josephines')? Do we make them feel judged as counterfeit, as fakes? Who in your life is always made to feel inadequate because of your over-confidence or self-righteousness?

St Benedict encouraged his monks to be open and available to all who arrived at the door of the monastery: 'The greatest care should be taken to give a warm reception to the poor and to pilgrims, because it is in them above all that Christ is welcomed.'

The poor; those low on self-esteem; and the pilgrim, the wanderer, those in search of God and of their real self, who we snootily dismiss as 'godless', making them feel 'judged counterfeit'. No wonder they resort, as a last throw of the dice, to retaliation. The root of the conflict is that the virtuous always have, and always have to have, the last word.

In each instance of growth in depth and sincerity of relationship, whether in the scripture story or in your own faith and life story, a moment of self-surrender embodies a meeting with Christ. It is that moment when we cease to be 'charitable' and instead become one with the poor. It is the moment when we realise that the nervous and uncertain pilgrim who knocks expectantly at the monastery door is closer to God than we are. It is that flicker of humility, self-knowledge and grace when we say, 'Let it be done to me according to your word', that becomes 'the sacrament of the present moment'.

At these moments, we and the poor and the pilgrim receive 'the greatest care and a warm welcome'.

Thought for the day

Why am I so skilled at noticing, and bringing to their attention, the splinter in my neighbour's eye whilst denying all knowledge of the plank in my own?

Prayer

Father, open our hearts to the voice of your Word
and free us from the darkness that shadows our vision.
Restore our sight that we may look fully towards repentance and a change of heart.
We ask this through Jesus Christ our Lord. Amen.

The Big Issue

Jr 11:18–20; Ps 7; Jn 7:40–52

> *'Let us destroy the tree in its strength, let us cut him off from the land of the living, so that his name may be quickly forgotten.'* (Jeremiah 11:19)

In the first reading, we read this tribute to the upright man, a foreshadowing of the fate of Christ, and the threat to us as disciples. Those who were challenged, in troubled or guilty conscience, by goodness and truth, seek to destroy, deny, disown, recognising the strength of the life and message of the believer.

The Church is *semper reformanda* (always reforming). Yet this mission statement is also one of its most closely guarded secrets. The gospel plots the life of the reformer, open-minded and warm-hearted; it also records the fate of those addicted to conformity, to set ritual. We face a choice. Lent is a time for decision. Do we choose to emerge into a faith of life, risk and adventure, or to defend a religion of effort, of resolutions, of gritted teeth and determination?

The gospel is full of individuals and groups scurrying about with blinkered vision and closed hearts, trying to plot Jesus's whereabouts and his person, oblivious to the reality that he lives among them. 'See for yourself', they say; 'prophets do not come out of Galilee' (John 7:52). But in fact we meet Christ in the places and in the people our prejudices tell us are the last places we would discover him. Prophets *do* come out of Galilee.

As we check and debate a stranger's credentials, as we note the asylum seeker's differences from us, as we pick holes in the case for debt relief, we fail to see Christ, in front of our nose. He is in the homeless person selling *The Big Issue*, he is in the woman in the CAFOD poster demanding justice for the poor.

One parishioner asked me some years ago, having listened to a homily: 'What is *The Big Issue*?'

It is a question for each of us this Lent.

Thought for the day

How many times have I met Christ today?

Prayer

Christ, the morning star,
when the night of this world is ended,
brings to your saints the promise of the light of life, and everlasting day. Amen.

Esther Mombo

Fifth Week of Lent

Fifth Sunday of Lent

Creating a new world

Jr 31:31–34; Ps 51, Heb 5:7–9, Jn 12:20–30

> *'Create in me a clean and pure heart, O God, and put a new and right spirit within me.'* (Psalm 51:10)

St Paul once summarised our encounter with Christ in the following words: 'The old has gone and the new has come …' (2 Corinthians 5:17). These are beautiful words, but if we try to interpret them they become baffling. What, we might want to ask, really is 'old' and what really is 'new'?

In the context of Paul's mission, the 'old' was his Jewish heritage with its uncompromising emphasis on the Law of Moses. The 'new' was the word of Christ. But even before Paul, Jeremiah had prophesied about a new covenant which would be different from the old covenant. The old covenant was exclusively for the Jewish people. They had to follow the law, which was to guide them especially in dealing with those who were weak and powerless. But they had broken this covenant and as a result they had been sent to exile. The new covenant, through Jesus Christ, would be for all people. The new law would be written in the hearts of the people. From now on, it was promised, people would relate to each other in a different way.

But look at the world around us. We still see human beings defined by their wealth, their ethnicity, their gender and their religion. Those who are poor and powerless continue to be marginalized. As a result, many people are turning away from religion. They look to money, or fame, or drugs as a source of comfort.

In the verses that follow today's gospel reading we hear that Jesus said, 'When am lifted up from the earth, I will draw all people to myself.' The mission and calling of the churches together is to usher in a bountiful new dispensation of abundant life. And the restoration of fragmented humanity starts with each of us, in a change of heart and mind and in a move to participate and to be involved.

Thought for the day

We do not wait for God to destroy this world and create a New World, but we co-operate with God to transform this present world and make it new.

Prayer

Lord have mercy upon us
when we stay fixed in the past and refuse to see what you have done to us through Jesus Christ.
Help us to usher in a new dispensation of abundant life to all in our society.
Give us insight today to see those whom we have excluded
and to share with them the joy we have in Jesus Christ. Amen.

Jesus escapes a trap

Dn 13:1–9, 15–17, 19–30; Ps 23; Jn 8:1–11

> *The scribes and Pharisees brought a woman along who had been caught committing adultery.* (John 8:1)

The law demanded the execution of both a man and a woman caught in adultery (Leviticus 20:10; Deuteronomy 22:22–24) but in today's gospel reading it is only the woman who faces trial. Why is this? First, it may be because of the discrimination against women in the male-dominated society of the time. Second, this woman is being set up as bait to trap Jesus, who was challenging the powerful of his day. Rome had removed capital jurisdiction from Jewish courts, except for temple violations. The Jewish leaders want to test whether Jesus would reject the law, so compromising his patriotic Jewish following, or reject the Roman rule, which would allow them to denounce him to the Romans.

Jesus does not fall into the trap. Instead he uses the Jewish law to give the people the final say on how they should deal with the woman. He asks the Pharisees to judge the woman using the same measure with which they would judge themselves: 'Let the one among you who is without sin be the first to throw a stone at her' (John 8:7). When they hear this, they leave one by one, until the woman is alone with Jesus. 'Neither do I condemn you', Jesus says to her. 'Go, and do not sin again' (v.10–11).

How full of encouragement this story is for victims of unjust interpretation of laws in our society. In places where legal systems defend women's rights only on paper, women who are commercial sex workers are rounded up and prosecuted whereas the men who trade with them are allowed to go free. As in the story of the woman caught in adultery, there always seems to be a double standard when judging men and women.

We must develop the same objectivity in discerning justice for men and women, for accusers and accused, that Jesus showed. And, to adapt the words of Jesus, those of us who are in the church must make ourselves personally accountable for our actions before we hold others accountable.

Thought for the day

Jesus put down the stone, and said, 'Neither do I condemn you'. When will the church put down its stones?

Prayer

Lord help us to rebuild broken and distorted lives
and to work towards building the living, thriving, just
community
that Jesus came to inaugurate. Amen.

The bronze serpent

Nb 21:4–9; Ps 102; Jn 8:21–30

> *'Why did you bring us out of Egypt to die in the desert? For there is neither food not water here.'*
>
> (Numbers 21:5)

Food and water are basic necessities of life. They are also a source of tension in our society. Where they are scarce there is tension. But even when they are available there is tension, because human beings do not share equally. There are those who will have and those who will not have.

In today's reading from Numbers the Jews on their way to Canaan are tired with the journey, and angry because there is scarcity of food and water. This has been their complaint from the time they left Egypt. Even when God provided for them they still complained. In this episode God is not amused with them and he punishes them by sending poisonous snakes to kill them. When they begin to die because of the poisonous snakes, Moses intercedes, and God provides healing for them. Moses is told to make a bronze serpent and to raise it up. Those who have been bitten who looked at it are healed.

Human beings are always complaining. Those who have so much always want more, and the have-nots wish for even a little of those who have. The horrendous disparity in our world between possession of the basic necessities of life such as food, water and shelter is a scandal. In many places, there is war and famine and disease because of the scarcity of food and water. Some use the scarcity of these basic needs to enrich themselves.

Some make the excuse that a scarcity of resources is inevitable, or the fault of the people themselves, or that there is nothing they can do to help.

We all deserve the wrath of God. We are saved only through Jesus Christ, who was lifted up on the cross like the bronze snake that Moses lifted up in the desert. Those who looked up at the bronze serpent were saved; and those who look up to Jesus on the cross will be forgiven their sins and will escape the wrath of God.

Thought for the day

If we are to avoid conflict in the world, a culture in which the endless accumulation of material possessions is regarded as normal has to be eroded by values such as self-restraint and simplicity and generosity.

Prayer

Make us worthy, Lord, to serve our fellow human beings throughout the world who live and die in poverty and hunger.
Through our hands grant them this day their daily bread;
and by our understanding love, give them peace and Joy.
Amen.

(Mother Teresa of Calcutta)

The Lord works through us

Dn 3:14–20, 24–28, 52–56; Jn 8:31–42

> *They walked in the heart of the flames, praising God and blessing the Lord.* (Daniel 3:24)

The story of Shadrach, Meshac and Abed-Nego is told with great dramatic skill. They were men of good standing in the community and might have been expected to set an example to others. But they paid no heed to King Nebuchadnezzar's decree that anyone who refused to worship the golden image would be thrown into a fiery furnace. They had made up their minds that they were not going to conform to the rule of idolatry and they were ready to pay the price for it.

The King was so furious with the three men that he ordered that the temperature of the furnace be raised to seven times its normal intensity. The heat was so severe that the guards who were to commit the offenders to the flames were burnt to death. But Shadrach, Meshac and Abed-Nego were seen walking freely in the heart of the fire by King Nebuchadnezzar, along with a fourth man 'who looked like the Son of the gods'. The King called Shadrach, Meshac and Abed-Nego out of the furnace. They did not even have a smell of fire on them. The King blessed the God of Israel and commended the young men for trusting in this God.

While this story gives strength to those in areas where the church is persecuted, it also puts demands on those of us who are privileged to live in easier circumstances. We should show how we value religious freedom by resisting any temptation to lethargy in our faith. At the same time we should pray for those who have to defend their faith each moment of their lives, and support those who live in countries where social injustice is so rampart that people have no space to worship God.

The Lord works through minds and wills like ours. If the will of God is going to be carried out it will only be through the co-operation of those who live in him, and through their determination to make society what God wants it to be. Christians have a responsibility in the world both for those who are free and those who are persecuted.

Thought for the day

Who can boast of being free? Who has not got secret prisons, invisible chains; all the more constricting the less they are apparent? (Dom Helder Camara)

Prayer

Dear God
help us to serve our fellow human beings who live and die in poverty and hunger.
Give them through our labours this day their daily bread
and by your understanding love, give us peace and joy as we serve you in this way. Amen.

Always with us

Gn 17:3–9, Ps 105; Jn 8:51–59

> *God said to Abraham, 'I shall bless Sarah and give you a son by her.'* (Genesis 17:16)

To have no heir put Sarah and Abraham in a very awkward position. For Sarah it was a double tragedy, because in this society her worth as a mother and wife was through giving birth, and as a barren woman her self-esteem was very low. Sarah had commanded Abraham to sleep with Hagar, the house girl, so that they could have an heir. But when Ishmael was born relationships in the family had gone sour.

When Sarah and Abraham received the promise of God about a son, they were both in their nineties. They faced a bleak future, they were desolate and powerless. The promise must have sounded like a dream to them, and this is why they both laughed. When Isaac was born Sarah said, 'God has given me good reason to laugh, and everybody who hears will laugh with me' (Genesis 21:6).

The situation of Jews in the time of Jesus was also hopeless, desolate. They were powerless under Roman rule. They could be compared to a barren couple whose destiny was bleak. They saw Jesus as their messiah and they hoped he would deliver them from the yoke of the Romans. But Jesus did not come to deliver them in the way they expected. They objected to the fact that he would link himself to their ancestor Abraham, and say that he existed before Abraham. This is why on one occasion they wanted to kill him with stones even before he was crucified.

The situation for many in some parts of our world is unbearable. Women often bear the brunt, the mothers in families who are landless, homeless and powerless. Can Christ be a saviour in such situations? People often resort to other ways of trying to survive. At times they turn to violence. Others turn to drugs and crime. When we think of the way to the cross we are reminded that those who follow Christ are not promised an easy time. But we are assured that he will be with us always. Christ suffers with all who suffer. He remains the hope of the world.

Thought for the day

Peace and love are always at work in us, but we are not always in peace and love. But Christ wants us in this way to realise that he is the foundation of the whole of our life in love, and furthermore that he is our eternal protector, and mighty defender against our enemies who are so very fierce and wicked. (Julian of Norwich)

Prayer

Dear God help us to realise that Christ suffered for us
and continues to suffer with us even when he is not here with us.
Give us grace to continue trusting you even in the midst of hardships. Amen.

The way of the non-conformist

Jr 20:10–13, Ps 18; Jn 10:31–42

The Jews fetched stones to stone him. (John 10:31)

There is no question that Jesus Christ was different. He did things that disconcerted both his friends and his enemies. To the Jews he did not confirm that he was the expected messiah, but said instead that he 'was from God who was his Father' and that 'the Father and I are one' (John 10:30). Jesus tried to show the Jews that his Father had appointed him; that whatever he was doing was not for his own glory, but for the glory of his Father. He was from the beginning of the world dedicated to be the meeting point between God and humanity, the one through whom humanity could approach God. But to the Jews this was blasphemy. He ignited their anger and they wanted to kill him, because he did not conform to what they wanted.

Christ the non-conformist, who always did things differently, either made it possible for people to get outside of themselves and to follow a different way, or led them to dig deeper into fixed positions, to take refuge behind indifference or outright animosity.

Christ, the strange nonconformist, forces each of us, too, to look at our strange conformities and make a choice. Which choice will it be? Do we reject as idealistic, impractical and insane the demands he makes; or do we attempt and keep on attempting to aspire and keep on aspiring toward the more excellent way?

To be a non-conformist for Christ's sake may not be easy. It is often uncomfortable socially and difficult spiritually. When we see victims of natural disasters or war on our TV screens we could easily switch off so that we are not disturbed by images of hunger and malnutrition. We may tell ourselves that the little we can offer will not help much. But who else can make a difference if not us?

Thought for the day

We are called upon to get involved and make things happen in the lives of those we care for.

Prayer

Lord Jesus you always did what your father expected you to do in all circumstances.
We ask you to enlighten our minds and strengthen our wills
so that we may know what we ought to do, and be enabled to do it through the grace of your Holy Spirit. Amen.

The valley of dry bones

Ezk 37:21–28; Jr 31:10–13; Jn 11:45–56

> *The Lord God says this to the dry bones: 'I am now going to make breath enter you, and you will live.'*
>
> (Ezekiel 37:4)

As a result of the HIV/AIDS pandemic whole communities are lost in hopelessness, despair and fear. In every part of the world, people have had to face up to the challenge of this pandemic. There are those who are dealing with the sick and the dying by providing the necessary care so that they are able to die in dignity. There are those who are dealing with the grieving relatives of the dead and helping them to come to terms with the loss. There are others who are dealing with the increasing number of orphans who are unable to fend for themselves. And as well as dealing with the tragic situations that arise directly from the pandemic, we need to discuss the problem openly, so that no-one is stigmatised, treatments are made available, and the rate of infections decreases.

In his vision the prophet Ezekiel sees a valley filled with dry bones. God asks, 'Can these bones live?' (Ezekiel 37:3). Ezekiel answers that it is only God who knows. Ezekiel is then told to prophesy. As he does so, the bones become covered with flesh and skin. Then he prophesies again, and breath enters them, and they come back to life and stand up on their feet.

The bones were a symbol of the Jews in exile after ten years; with Jerusalem destroyed they had no hope. They were like the valley of dry bones, and Ezekiel was bringing a message of hope to them. And just as the bones came to life in two stages, so the restoration of Israel was to be in two stages: first, the partial restoration and second, the full restoration.

The situation of the HIV/AIDS pandemic in the world can be seen as like that of the valley of dry bones. This is almost literally the case in some parts of Africa, where villages are deserted or are inhabited only by old people and orphans. In other parts of the world, many are numb to the realities of Africa. Is there any hope in this desolate situation? Can this space of death and hopelessness be transformed?

The answer of the Christian gospel is that, Yes, with Christ and the way of the cross, the apparently hopeless situation can be transformed. Like the valley of dry bones, it will take two stages. First, with the support of those who act like Ezekiel and 'prophesy life', those affected by HIV/AIDS can be helped to live with dignity. Second, it is the role of all of us to make poverty history, to create a just world in which everyone is brought fully to life, and stands up on their feet.

Thought for the day

As Christ identified with our suffering and enters into it, so the church as the body of Christ is called to enter into the suffering of others, to stand with them against all rejection and despair.

Prayer

Oh God we are almost without hope
we are weighed down, infected and affected with HIV/AIDS,
subject to stigma and discrimination.
You who transformed the valley of dry bones
bring our societies fully to life. Amen.

Margaret Hebblethwaite

Holy Week and Easter Sunday

Passion (Palm) Sunday

A king who embraces poverty

Is 50:4–7; Ps 22; Ph 2:6–11; Mk 14:1—15:47

> *'You always have the poor with you, and you can show kindness to them whenever you wish; but you will not always have me.'* (Mark 14:7)

Holy Week begins with the reading of the Passion from the gospel of the year, which is Mark. On Good Friday we will hear the Passion read again in John's version. Reading through Mark's two chapters gives us an overview of what is to come, and reminds us of all that was in Jesus' mind as he made that triumphant yet fatal entry into Jerusalem. It was a victory parade, but of a king who rode on a donkey instead of in a magnificent chariot, and who passed through an arch of palm branches instead of a stone triumphal arch like Marble Arch or the Arc de Triomphe. That is the kind of king we have, a king who was poor and whose courtiers were poor – a king who turned all the usual worldly values upside down.

The Passion story begins with the anointing of Jesus at Bethany. This was a highly significant act, to which we customarily pay too little attention. The very word 'Christ' means 'Anointed One', so here we have a key moment at which Jesus was consecrated to be the kind of Messiah he was to be – a Messiah who was to save the people by his death. And, true to form, he was formally consecrated to this holy office not by any priest or religious authority but by someone anonymous, lay and female. The woman whose momentous act was destined to be 'told in remembrance of her, wherever the good news is proclaimed in the whole world', does not even have a name.

What is more, the solemn anointing takes place not in any consecrated building but in the house of a leper, the most despised and rejected grouping of people because of their deformities and the risk of contagion. The King of the Jews has humbled himself to the level of the bottom of society, and in the process lifts up the people at the bottom. The rejected people now become the holy people, the new priesthood.

When Jesus says, 'You always have the poor with you, and you can show kindness to them whenever you wish; but you will not always have me', he is telling us that we can go on honouring and cherishing him whenever we wish after he has gone, simply by honouring and cherishing the poor. What we give to the poor, we give to Jesus.

Thought for the day

Good perfume is expensive to buy, but it is made from the beautiful smells that are free – the scent of blossoms in the air and of spicy plants that you can crush in your fingers.

Prayer

Sweet Jesus, you loved the poor and made yourself one
of them.
Take me with you in your humility this holy week,
so that afterwards I may find you in your poor sisters
and brothers. Amen.

Giving thanks

Is 42:1–7; Ps 27; Jn 12:1–11

> *Mary brought in a pound of very costly ointment, and with it anointed the feet of Jesus.* (John 12:3)

This year we are allowed to dwell in more detail on the important mystery of the anointing, because we have it on two consecutive days. But today's gospel from John is not just a repetition of Mark's version: it has some markedly different features, which give us a new angle on the same event.

One of the most striking differences is that Mark tells us how the head of Jesus was covered with the oil, but John tells us that his feet were anointed. The anointing of the head is the solemn event by which kings were anointed (see 1 Samuel 10:1 and 16:1). But the anointing of the feet is a more sensuous act, in which the woman massages the oil lovingly into Jesus' feet and wraps them up in her own hair.

Another of the major differences gives us a clue to the meaning of this act: yesterday's woman was anonymous, but today's woman has a name. She is Mary of Bethany, the sister of Lazarus, and her sensuous act is her way of saying an extravagant Thank-you for freeing her brother from the power of death.

Lazarus is not the only person to be freed from the power of death. We all share in that liberation, even though we have not physically died yet. So Mary becomes a figure for us, and we can join ourselves with her to adore the feet of Jesus with our body, mind and spirit. We join with her in thanking him with all our hearts for what he has done for us, and will do for us this week.

Giving thanks is a hugely important part of human relations, and we feel that need all the more keenly when the relationship appears on the face of it unequal: parents to children, healthy to sick, rich to poor. When someone gives us a gift, we want to give one back again, and when that is not possible we may have to make do with words alone. One young girl in Santa María de Fe, Paraguay, where I live, wanted to give her boyfriend a present for his birthday, but she was poor and had nothing she could give. So she just wrote him a letter, telling him how much he meant to her. It was the best gift she could have given, and shortly afterwards they were married.

Thought for the day

Giving thanks gives dignity to the person who receives a gift, because it makes the relationship one of mutual giving and receiving.

Prayer

Thank you, Jesus, for giving me life, and freedom, and friendship.
Show me your sisters and brothers,
so that I may pour out my love for you in gifts to them. Amen.

Peter's tears

Is 49:1–6; Ps 71; Jn 13:21–33, 36–38

> *'Before the cock crows, you will have denied me three times.'* (John 13:38)

After the faithful Mary of Bethany, we pick up the stories of two of the male disciples who disgraced themselves this week. Today we anticipate the Last Supper, and Jesus' distress as he warns that one of the inner twelve, Judas, is to betray him, and another, Peter, is to deny him. We will come back to Judas tomorrow, but for now let's reflect on Peter's infidelity.

Peter is so certain his love of Christ will keep him faithful. Why, he is even prepared to die for Jesus! But Jesus tells him, 'Before the cock crows, you will have denied me three times.' As we know, this is exactly what happened. Peter meant well – he lied in an attempt to stay close to Jesus, infiltrating the high priest's house. He had not accepted Jesus' warning that 'Where I am going, you cannot follow me now.' And when he discovered that following Jesus physically had led him to abandon Jesus spiritually, he went out and wept bitterly.

In the depths of the Paraguayan campo, where I live, there is a wonderful statue commemorating this moment of Peter's tears. It was carved out of wood by the Guaraní indigenous in the late seventeenth or early eighteenth century, and stands nearly head-high. Peter has his head tilted upwards to catch the cockcrow, and his right forefinger lifted to show that he is attending to the sound and recognising its implications. Four or five painted tears trickle from his each of his eyes.

It is an unusual theme that the Guaraní have captured, but it says a great deal to us. We can identify with Peter because we too are sinners, we too mean well but make hopeless miscalculations, we too want to listen in this holy week, to attend, to pray, to make statements of faithful love that will not prove false promises.

Peter wept, but he found his reconciliation with his beloved master when they breakfasted together on the beach in John 21. Just as he had denied three times being Jesus' friend, he now had the opportunity to affirm three times that yes, he was his friend, that he loved him. It was the most beautiful, gentle way of making things right again.

Thought for the day

Praying is listening to God: often we need to listen to the sounds of creation to hear the voice of the Spirit.

Prayer

Be gentle with me, Jesus, when I am in tears and it's my own fault.
Be understanding, and give me another chance,
just as you did with Peter. Amen.

The story of Judas

Is 50:4–9; Ps 69; Mt 26:14–25

> *'Alas for that man by whom the Son of man is betrayed.'* (Matthew 26:24)

Judas' story, unlike Peter's, does not end with a reconciliation. We do not know quite why Judas betrayed Jesus, but if he really did it for the money, we may presume that he thought Jesus would talk his way out of this one, just as he had talked his way out of every awkward incident up till now. The money was enough to purchase a field, so it must have been worth quite a lot. Perhaps Judas thought it would be a clever way of making money, without putting his supposedly invulnerable master at real risk.

It is clear that Judas never expected things to turn out the way they did, or he would never have gone back to the chief priests – as we learn in Matthew 27:3 – to declare himself a sinner, throw down the ill-gotten money, and go off and hang himself. He would not have done that unless he loved Jesus hugely, so much that he felt he could never live with himself afterwards because of what he had done. He thought there was nothing he could ever do, no penance no matter how great, that could make up for a mortal sin (that is, a death-dealing sin) of such enormity as his.

The evangelists speak of Judas with bitterness and John called him a 'thief' in Monday's gospel. Yet Jesus never condemns Judas. When he says in today's gospel, 'Woe to that one by whom the Son of Humanity is betrayed: it would have been better for him not to have been born,' he is not uttering a curse upon him, but commiserating with Judas' appallingly awful situation.

The truth is that since Jesus poured out his blood for the forgiveness of sins, it is not necessary to feel that we cannot be forgiven unless we can make up for what we have done wrong. Nothing Judas could ever do would ever make up for his sin. But that does not matter, because someone else made up for it instead of him. Since the death of Jesus, there will never again be need in the world for capital punishment. The death penalty has already been paid.

Thought for the day

The poor and the rich stand on equal terms when it comes to paying compensation for wrongdoing: the life of Jesus is given for all of us.

Prayer

Lift from me, Jesus, the bitterness I feel at times.
You were not bitter because of what Judas did,
because you never lost sight of him as a brother. Amen.

Our wedding ring

Ex 12:1–8, 11–14; Ps 116; 1 Co 11:23–26; Jn 13:1–15

> *'I have given you an example so that you may copy what I have done to you.'* (John 13:15)

'This cup is the new covenant', says Jesus. In Spanish, the language of most countries of South America, the word for 'covenant' is *alianza*, and the same word also means 'wedding ring'. So if we speak in Spanish we do not run the risk of people saying 'What does "covenant" mean?'. It is an everyday reality, because it is a ring on the finger, an easy tangible sign of a permanent commitment.

God's promise to us in the Eucharist is something we can touch and taste – something as tangible as the wedding ring. We do not sign up to this contract by reading a document and signing our name: that is only the way that educated people use when they make covenants. The poor are disadvantaged in such legal agreements, because they do not understand all the long words and are often confused and baffled, and sometimes even deceived.

No, God does not favour the educated. The covenant made with God's people is made as simply as by eating a bit of bread and drinking from a common cup. Anyone can do it. Even a child. Even a person with learning difficulties. Receiving communion means a great deal even to those who cannot articulate what it is that it means.

In South America many people cannot afford to buy a gold wedding ring. In Santa María de Fe most people borrow a ring from the parish for their wedding ceremony, but do not go home with it. In other communities, a black ring made of coconut wood is used, instead of gold. The great Brazilian Bishop Pedro Casaldáliga popularised the use of this black ring by missionaries and pastoral workers, so that in many South American countries it has now become a regular sign of commitment to the people, a pledge of working with and for the poor.

In other words, it is our *alianza*, our covenant, the covenant we can share in because Jesus first made it with us on Maundy Thursday at his Last Supper. And Jesus alone can give the strength to be faithful to it.

Thought for the day

Drinking from a common cup is an everyday act in Paraguay, where the traditional drinks of *mate* and *tereré* are always handed around and drunk from a common metal straw. To wipe it before drinking would be very rude.

Prayer

I want to be faithful to your values, Jesus,
but I have so many other desires that I'm not sure I can make it if the going gets tough.
Come and live in me, so that I will want more of what you want, and less of what I want. Amen.

Sharing in the death of the poor

Is 52:13–53:12; Ps 31; Heb 4:14–16, 5:7–9; Jn 18:1—19:42

Pilate handed him over to be crucified. (John 18:16)

In Paraguay, under the 35-year dictatorship of General Alfredo Stroessner (1954–1989), there were two quite different ways of dealing with dissidents. Those who might raise an international outcry were expelled from the country: they included a number of Spanish Jesuits, and the world-famous Paraguayan novelist Augusto Roa Bastos. But if you were just a poor *campesino* who would pass unnoticed, then you were imprisoned, tortured, and possibly tortured to death.

Jesus shares in this death of the poor, despite his huge reputation. He dies like the poor. Indeed, he dies like a criminal. He is utterly humiliated. He is tortured to death.

Jesus does not go through his passion scoring verbal points against his opponents, like a sort of James Bond figure in chains. He maintains a silence in his two trials – with the high priest and then with Pilate. He only gives non-committal answers like, 'Why ask me? Ask my hearers', and, 'It is you who say it'.

As the prophecy from Isaiah says, 'He never opened his mouth, like a lamb that is led to the slaughter-house.' By opting to identify with the powerless and dying like a nobody, he ensures that nothing of the pain of humanity passes him by.

Pain is a great leveller. Fine thoughts go out of your head when you are in pain, and the only thing you can think of is the pain. Jesus was in pain, not yet physical torment as he would be on the cross, but still a deep pain that those he loved so much had turned against him. As the Good Friday hymn says:

> Why, what hath my Lord done?
> What makes this rage and spite?
> He made the lame to run,
> He gave the blind their sight.

In Santa María we have a moving wooden statue, carved by the Guaraní indigenous, of Jesus at the pillar after his scourging. His hurt eyes say it all: a silent hurt that cannot find words but just looks straight at you and sees into your very soul.

Thought for the day

The gospels have few words for the horror of the cross. Instead of piling on the descriptions of the physical torture, they simply say 'They crucified him', and leave it at that. There are some things too terrible to speak about.

Prayer

O Jesus, you are without words at this moment.
I am without words too, as I don't know what to say that would be adequate.
Hold me in your gaze, so that I can go on holding you in my gaze.

The resurrection of the poor

Rm 6:3–11; Ps 117; Mk 16:1–7

> *'Very early in the morning, on the first day of the week ...'* (Mark 16:2)

Getting up just before dawn, to get in every possible hour of work while there is light, is the daily routine in poor rural communities. Dawn is a surprisingly noisy time, with the singing of birds and the cocking of crows, with occasional sound additions from pigs, horses and dogs. But it is a quiet time too, in the sense that peasants will sit very still and drink maté, as a sort of morning meditation.

We lose that early-morning-with-nature feeling in the developed world, where we have adapted to the lazier rhythm of rising some hours after dawn, and staying up for several artificially lit hours after dusk. But a few people choose to get up especially early on Easter Sunday morning, to live through with Mary of Magdala and her companions the glory of the rising Sun.

'Who will roll away the stone for us?' ask the women. The huge, heavy stone symbolises the back-breaking work of so many in the world, and the burdens they can scarcely bear. The Jesuit martyr-theologian from El Salvador, Ignacio Ellacuría, used to call the poor 'the crucified peoples', and this idea is echoed in today's epistle by St Paul. 'Our former selves have been crucified with him', he says, and 'we have imitated his death'.

So this night's rising is also the resurrection of the poor. 'As Christ was raised from the dead by the Father's glory', so too do the crucified peoples inherit a new life.

At first it is strange and unbelievable, even a bit frightening. And they do not see the resurrection straight away. But what they are told to do is to get walking. 'He is going before you to Galilee; it is there you will see him.'

Migrants – those who walk to new places to seek work – and pilgrims – those who walk to new places to seek God – are given the promise that Christ is ahead of them. He is not behind them, trying to catch up, but ahead there at the end, drawing them to him and giving speed to their journey.

Thought for the day

Mary of Magdala brings spices to anoint the body of Jesus but, as we saw on Palm Sunday, the body of Jesus was 'anointed beforehand for its burial' by another woman. Mary of Magdala is given a new role: not to anoint the dead but to proclaim the resurrection as the first Easter witness.

Prayer

Draw me to you,
my Hope and my Joy,
and let me see your Glory. Amen.

At one with the poor

Ac 10:34, 37–43; Ps 117; Col 3:1–4; Jn 20:1–9

He saw and he believed. (John 20:8)

When something important has happened, we want to hear the account over and over, told by different people, in case we glean a little more information each time. John's account of the empty tomb tells us about the visit of Peter and the beloved disciple. Many people believe that the beloved disciple is the evangelist John himself, which would explain why this story reads like an eyewitness account: 'I got there first but I didn't go in. He came after, but he was first to go in and he saw. So I went in too and looked, and that is when I understood.'

One of the beautiful and intriguing aspects of this account is how faith comes through observation of clothing. As a matter of everyday experience, we often recognise who people are by what they are wearing. Even apart from those who wear special clothes for their profession, like a police officer or a nurse, we instantly sum up the background, wealth and educational level of anyone we meet by taking one look at their clothes. They do not even need to open their mouth.

Jesus is a king, and kings usually wear rich clothes and occasionally a crown. He is a prophet, and prophets may wear rugged unconventional clothes or even animal skins. He is a priest, and priests are often expected to put on black suits with a stand-up white collar when they are not in liturgical vestments.

Jesus does not wear any of these things. On the contrary, he is recognised as the Risen Son of God from items of clothing that are so humble that only the dead wear them: a shroud and a binding cloth for the head. Peter and the beloved disciple come to faith because they see these items of clothing, see that they are empty, and see how they are lying – the shroud cast on the ground, and the binding cloth neatly rolled up apart. Quite why this positioning was so significant for them is not the point: the point is that when they saw that, then they knew who and what Jesus was – that he was the risen Christ victorious over death.

Once again, in his use of decisive clothing, Jesus opts to make himself one with the poorest of the poor, with those who have nothing at all, because they have lost everything in death.

Thought for the day

In this world of reversed values, those with shining new clothes are the ones who have washed them white in the blood of the Lamb. (Revelation 7:13).

Prayer

You told Thomas,
'Happy are those who have not seen and yet believe.'
Open my eyes to see the significance of little things,
and so find you without dramatic demonstrations.
Amen.

About CAFOD

CAFOD is the Catholic Agency for Overseas Development. It is the official overseas development and relief agency of the Catholic Church in England and Wales. CAFOD has been fighting poverty in developing countries since 1962.

CAFOD believes that all human beings have a right to dignity and respect, and that the world's resources are a gift to be shared equally by all men and women, whatever their race, nationality or religion.

CAFOD is a member of the Caritas International Federation, a worldwide network of Catholic relief and development organisations.

CAFOD raises funds from the Catholic community in England and Wales, the UK government and the general public so that it can:

- promote long-term development, helping people in need to bring about change for themselves through development and relief work.
- respond to emergencies, providing immediate help for people affected by conflict or natural disasters.
- identify the causes of poverty and raise public awareness of them, encouraging supporters and the public to challenge the structures, policies and attitudes that reinforce inequality.
- speak out on behalf of poor communities, explaining the underlying causes of poverty and challenging governments and international bodies to adopt policies that promote equality and justice.

- promote human development and social justice in witness to Christian faith and gospel values.

Enacting Gospel values

CAFOD's work is one of the ways in which the Church expresses and enacts its belief in human dignity and social justice.

It is inspired by Scripture ('to bring good news to the poor,' Luke 4:18), by Catholic Social Teaching and by the experiences and hopes of the poor, marginalised and often oppressed communities it supports.

It works to enact Gospel values – within and beyond the Church – including:

- concern for our neighbours and the wellbeing of future generations
- serving the common good to enable everyone to develop equally
- fighting for social justice and ensuring everyone's basic needs are met
- acting on the basis of need, not greed, and acting in solidarity with those living in poverty
- promoting the values of human dignity, community, stewardship and the integrity of creation.

CAFOD puts into practice the solidarity and communion for which the Church stands, and strives for a world built on interdependence, mutuality and sharing, where exclusion, exploitation and greed do not exist.

Website: www.cafod.org.uk

About Christian Aid

In 1945, the British and Irish churches created Christian Aid to put faith into action amid the ruins of a horrific war. Sixty years on, we work with church partners, the ecumenical family and sister agencies as well as with alliances of other faiths and secular groups which share our passionate determination to end poverty.

Christian Aid works wherever the need is greatest – irrespective of religion or race.

Because we believe in strengthening people to find their own solutions to the problems they face, we support local organisations, which are best placed to understand local needs. We also give help on the ground through 16 overseas offices.

Christian Aid Week each year is the largest house-to-house collection in the UK, with the involvement of over 300,000 volunteers and 20,000 local churches and committees.

We strive for a new world transformed by an end to poverty and we campaign to change the rules that keep people poor.

Our values

The essential purpose of Christian Aid is to expose the scandal of poverty, to help in practical ways to root it out from the world, and to challenge and change the systems which favour the rich and powerful over the poor and marginalised.

Put life first
We believe that all people are created equal, with inherent dignity and infinite worth. Individual human needs must always come first, ahead of dogma, ideology or political necessity. We know that each one of us, in all our diversity and varied talents, can make a real difference in the battle to end poverty and injustice.

Struggle for justice
Poverty is a condition created by an unjust society, denying people access to, and control over, the resources they need to live a full life.

So we take the side of poor and marginalised people as they struggle to realise their civil, political, economic, social and cultural rights.

We believe in the just and sustainable use of the earth and its resources, so that the greed of one generation will not create poverty for the next.

Speak out courageously
We have a duty to speak out and act with conviction to challenge and change the systems that create poverty.

Christian Aid always remains independent of governments and other powerful institutions. We work to educate and mobilise people from all kinds of backgrounds to build a global movement which can change the course of history.

Test everything against experience
We know that poor people are the true experts on the nature of poverty, and our work is shaped by their voices and concerns.

In a spirit of humility, we try to learn from our own mistakes and from the experience of those we work alongside, to improve the impact of our work.

We know that lasting solutions can never be imposed on communities from the outside.

Work together with others

All our work is based on the spirit of cooperation and partnership. We help to build a world free from poverty through inter-faith and intercommunity dialogue and cooperation.

We nurture the talents, commitment and energy of all our supporters, volunteers and staff. Together we uphold a commitment to honesty, mutual respect, accountability and diversity.

Towards a new earth

For Christian Aid this is a time to act upon our dream of a new earth on which we all stand equally, to renew our faith and hope, to reaffirm our commitment to the world's poorest communities, and to promote the dignity and rights of people throughout the world.

Website: www.christian-aid.org.uk